A GIVING SPIRIT

THE STORY OF
PAUL W. BRANDEL

A GIVING Spirit

THE STORY OF PAUL W. BRANDEL

Covenant Benevolent Institutions, Inc.
5145 North California Avenue
Chicago, Illinois 60625

ISBN 0-9626063-0-8
Copyright © 1990 by Covenant Benevolent Institutions, Inc.
Design and layout: David Westerfield
Production: Covenant Publications

To the glory of God
and the memory of Paul W. Brandel
1911-1986

"For where your treasure is,
there will your heart be also."
Matthew 6:21

CONTENTS

FOREWORD

Paul Brandel was more than a generous layman: he was a Christian phenomenon. Husband, father, attorney, venture capitalist, traveler, church leader, and philanthropist, his influence reached around the globe and spanned more than half a century.

The impact of lay leadership on the progress of God's kingdom is often heralded but seldom chronicled. This is largely due to the fact that church history is written mostly about the clergy, on behalf of the clergy, and by the clergy.

How delightful to see a book that tells the story of an unforgettable lay leader!

I first met Paul thirty years ago when I was pastoring my first church. An irascible and fascinating older woman wanted to donate a lovely piece of property to build a retirement center near my church. I was put in touch with Covenant Board of Benevolence president Nils G. Axelson. Nils quickly showed up, along with Paul Brandel.

Then followed a quarter-century of friendship that included Paul's participation in my wedding in 1966 and ended with his sudden death soon after I moved to Chicago to become president of the Covenant.

I worked with him over the years, as did many others, in his aggressive and immensely successful efforts in building a group of splendid retirement centers across the nation. Together with Nils Axelson, he turned a single small home for the elderly into the nation's fifth largest nonprofit organization of retirement communities.

Time and again, Paul would place his fortune at risk to ensure that the work would go forward. This he did because he believed that no Christian should put Christ's work at risk unless that person put his or her personal fortune at risk as well. And all of this he did while also helping our two acute-care hospitals, our college and seminary, our missions work, as well as countless organizations and philanthropies that reached far beyond the small confines of our denomination. Yet he maintained his legal practice and numerous business enterprises, the largest of which was his work in partnership with A. Harold Anderson in one of the most successful industrial real-estate development firms in the Midwest.

Paul was always fun to be around. He enjoyed a boisterous and contentious debate—which made us most compatible. I remember getting into a heated argument on politics on a flight from San Francisco to Santa Barbara. It got louder and louder until Paul finally burst out laughing. The entire cabin of the aircraft had turned its attention to our debate!

Once we were asked to consult on a retirement project of another denomination. He gathered ten wealthy laymen in southern California for lunch. Most of them had no connection with the project. He simply explained the need to raise one million dollars immediately. Since he was leading the meeting, he said he would contribute the first $100,000. With an impish gleam in his eye, he then went around the circle asking each one personally if he could afford to do the same. There was coughing and groaning—but all ten agreed within two minutes. This was the quickest raising of a million dollars that I have ever seen.

This generosity was not born of affluence. Paul told me once that when he first began his law practice, he had to clean offices in downtown Chicago in order to make ends meet. One evening he attended a missionary meeting at the Ravenswood Covenant Church. He was so moved by the message that he emptied his pockets. He gave the entire $50 he had in the offering. As he left the church, it suddenly occurred to him that he had given his last cent on earth. He had not one dollar on which to live and support his wife and infant daughter for the next two weeks. Needless to say, they never went hungry!

Of even more significance was his love for Christ and for people of modest circumstance. His heart always warmed to the preaching of the Gospel. He would travel far and long to remember the birthday of an elderly friend or to visit a retired employee. Much of his giving to people in need was known only to the recipients, and many times they did not know that it was he who aided them. He remembered the words of Jesus, "Do not give so that your giving may be seen of men. . . ."

I could write a book about my adventures with Paul Brandel. But I don't have to because others have done it in what follows! May this book entertain you, move you, and change you!

Paul E. Larsen, *President*
The Evangelical Covenant Church
Chicago, Illinois

PREFACE

In the weeks and months following my husband's death on June 30, 1986, I received hundreds of letters from people all over the country, not only expressing their sympathy but relating stories of how Paul had helped them or influenced their lives in some way.

Although I had known Paul most of my life and had worked for him for thirty years and been married to him for the last eleven years of his life, many of these stories were new to me—known only to God and to the persons affected. I was continually amazed at how Paul had touched so many lives. I often wondered how one person could cram so much into a lifespan of seventy-four years.

Soon people began to suggest that a book be written about him. The first to make this suggestion was Jim Aspegren, for many years administrator of Covenant Village of Northbrook, where we made our home. The Rev. Karl Johnson of Princeton, Illinois, also encouraged the project, believing that the story of Paul's stewardship could be an inspiration for pastors, laypersons, and young people to carry on the Paul Brandel legacy.

I am indebted to Nils G. Axelson, president of Covenant Benevolent Institutions, for getting this project launched and for his strong belief that the story of our outstanding leaders in The Evangelical Covenant Church should be preserved for future generations.

Finally, I am grateful to the chapter writers in this book. Each one responded most enthusiastically to our request, and there are many more we could have asked.

I think Paul would be surprised and humbled to know that his singleminded desire to give to the Lord's work would result in a book. I think he would enjoy a good many chuckles reading it. But I also think it would inspire him to give even more generously—and that's what he would hope this book will do for you.

Bernice Brandel
Northbrook, Illinois

INTRODUCTION

Paul William Brandel was born in Chicago on October 7, 1911, to Christine and Carl Brandel, Swedish immigrants who first settled on the South Side of Chicago. When Paul was twelve, his father, a builder, brought the family to the North Side, where they lived at several different addresses.

He would often arrange first and second mortgages on the apartments he was building, and when the Depression hit, he lost everything except the house they lived in. This experience affected Paul deeply. His father's strong conviction that your earthly goods can be taken away anytime and that "only what you give away lasts," coupled with their pastor's persuasive stewardship sermons, determined the pattern for Paul Brandel's future.

Paul graduated from North Park Academy in 1928 and from North Park Junior College in 1930. He continued his education at Chicago Kent College of Law, graduating in 1933. He was admitted to both the Chicago and Illinois bar associations.

His father's sudden death in the fall after his law-school graduation thrust him into the role of sole supporter of the family, with their home about to be foreclosed. For several struggling years, he shared office space downtown with other lawyers and also hung his sign in the window of a North-Side moving company to try to attract Swedish clientele.

His practice prospered and continued for more than half a century, based for many years in downtown Chicago and later in Northbrook, Illinois. As the years passed, he turned to real-estate investment and teamed with others in successful ventures of many kinds. As president of Paul W. Brandel Enterprises, he became known for his visionary business instincts and willingness to take risks.

Through the years, the Brandels were active members of Covenant churches in the Chicago and suburban areas where they lived—Ravenswood, Edgebrook, and Northbrook. A leader in the denomination, Paul Brandel held one of its highest offices—chairman of the Trustees.

His interest in Covenant Benevolent Institutions began in the 1930s when he was elected to its board for the first of many terms. Over the years, he gave land and financial assistance totaling millions of dollars, as well as his tireless dedication to the development of six Covenant Retirement Communities in Florida, California, and Illinois. As a result, residents in comfortable retirement centers around the country enjoy a beautiful lifestyle unheard of in earlier times. Several facilities at these centers are named for Paul Brandel.

He served on the boards of numerous financial, educational, cultural, and charitable organizations. Endowed chairs in nursing and in New Testament studies at North Park College and Theological Seminary bear his name. He received several honorary doctorates and numerous awards, including special recognition by the Covenant Centennial Annual Meeting, receiving the Commander of the Royal Order of the North Star award from the king of Sweden, and being listed in *Who's Who in the World.*

His first wife, Vega Rundquist, whom he married in 1938, died in 1970. They had one daughter, Carola, who, with her husband, Loren Anderson, lives in Sun Prairie, Wisconsin, and two grandchildren, Robert and Kristine. On January 3, 1976, Paul married Bernice Peterson Stege, who resides at Covenant Village of Northbrook.

Paul Brandel died on June 30, 1986, at the age of seventy-four. As the chapters in this book attest, what he gave away still lasts, and what he proclaimed in his own unique philosophy of living abides in the hearts of many people whose lives he resolutely influenced.

Eloise V. Nelson
Chicago, Illinois

PAUL BRANDEL'S LIVING PHILOSOPHY

Given on November 23, 1975, at the Chicago Sunday Evening Club.

I believe that faith is the substance of things hoped for, the evidence of things not seen (Hebrews 11:1). Faith is not trying to believe something regardless of the consequences. In my life, faith has played a very, very important part, and, as a result, I have a philosophy which has made me a great believer in the three T's of life—time, talent, and treasure. Every person has twenty-four hours a day, his own talent or ability, and the treasure he has been blessed with. His use of the three T's is the most important single factor in his life. It is essential to every Christian as a part of his philosophy of life that he be fully committed to the use of his time, his talent, and his treasure to the work of the Lord.

TIME. I believe a third of my time should be used in the charitable aspects of my life. William Allen White, on his seventieth birthday said, "I am not afraid of tomorrow, for I have seen yesterday and I love today." The right use of my time in the service of my church, my community, and my Lord has brought rewards far beyond my ability to comprehend. Is a part of your philosophy of life the gift of one-third of your time to your Lord? For every action, there is an equal, opposite reaction. If you want to receive much, you first have to give much. If each individual will give of himself to whomever he can, wherever he can, in any way that he can, in the long run he will be compensated in the exact proportion that he gives. What will be your compensation?

TALENT. My talents are dedicated to my church and the Lord it represents. What talents do you have? How do you use them? Are you like the servant with one talent who buried it, or the servant with five talents who increased them? We must use our talents where they will serve best. My father was a carpenter, and he invested his carpenter's abilities in helping others in that way. I am unable to handle a hammer, and so my talents are in other directions. Each person's talents are equally important; each must be used properly to make the whole. Christ moves through his servants' talents. Will you let him use yours?

TREASURE. In Matthew 6:21 we read, "Where your treasure is, there will your heart be also." Many of us are prone to criticize a person who is generous in his giving, but B. C. Forbes in his *Thoughts on the Business of Life* says the following: "Generosity and philanthropy are not inspired by the extent of your bank account. Unselfishness springs rather from your heart or disposition. Anyone who has not learned the job of contributing when he or she has not a superabundance, he or she is not likely to part with anything, no matter how their bank account may expand."

What is the joy in your giving? Have you learned when you have little to give from your heart because you are in Christ and all that you have is his, or is your giving a miserly act? Expand in your giving, and your whole life expands with it. Let us strive to give our time, talent, and treasure to Christ—a third of each. Keep in mind that where your treasure is, there your heart is also.

Theodore Roosevelt said: "Far better it is to dare mighty things, to win glorious triumphs, even though checkered by failure, than to take rank with those poor spirits who neither enjoy much or suffer much, because they live in the gray twilight that knows not victory nor defeat."

The unselfish contribution of time, talent, and treasure, as a part of my philosophy of life, has paid great dividends. Only that which I give away will last for eternity. I have tried to give a third of my time, whatever of my talents are usable at the moment they are required, and a third of my treasure so that I have really learned the joy of contributing. The first twenty years of life, I had a Christian father and mother teaching me. The next twenty years I learned something, the next twenty I earned something, and now in the last twenty years of my life, I will give away what the Lord has entrusted to me. My philosophy is one-third of my time, one-third of my talents, and one-third of my treasure in the work of my church and my Lord and Savior, who has provided opportunities, accomplishments, and rewards far beyond my greatest expectations.

"Give, and it will be given to you; good measure, pressed down, shaken together, running over, will be put into your lap. For the measure you give will be the measure you get back" (Luke 6:38).

Billy Graham has said, "God has given us two hands—one to receive with, and the other to give with. We are not cisterns made for hoarding—we are channels made for sharing." Won't you join me in being a fully committed Christian? Just keep on giving as long as the Lord keeps giving to you.

THE SEEDS ARE PLANTED

NORMA BRANDEL GIBBS

Norma Brandel Gibbs, a cousin of Paul Brandel, is associate professor of educational psychology at California State University, Long Beach, California.

My memories of Paul go back my entire lifetime. He was fourteen years older than I, and my first memory of him was at family get-togethers—usually big Sunday dinners after church in the home of one of the Brandel brothers.

Paul's father, Carl, and my father, David, were brothers. I would love to listen to them and another brother, Ephraim, tell and retell stories from their childhood in Värmland, Sweden. Their formal schooling ended at about the fourth grade, and they went to work to help on the farm or in the family business. Grandpa Brandel owned a soft-drink business. They made, bottled, and delivered the beverage. Dad would relate how as a child of twelve he had to lift heavy barrels and roll them into the shops. He would shake his head thinking about how much was expected of him at such a young age. When the building burned to the ground, all the boys had to find other employment.

Carl was the first brother to come to the United States, and Ephraim soon followed. They both settled on the South Side of Chicago, while my father stayed in Sweden to help the family. The youngest of eight children, he was reluctant to leave his mother alone. Finally, at the age of twenty-eight, unable to find employment near his home and with his dad working in Norway, his mother urged him to join his brothers in "the promised land."

All three brothers adored their mother and extolled her virtues endlessly. She must have been a saint, and apparently this feeling was shared by others, for she was described and even written up as a very generous, open-hearted woman who welcomed wayfarers with open arms. She also held church meetings in her home. I believe that the adoration the brothers had for their mother was transferred to their wives, for I never heard any of them ever say a cross word to or about them. None of the wives was allowed to work outside the home. It was enough for them to tend the household and see that the children were raised in a tranquil, God-fearing household, with great emphasis on church involvement and getting an education.

When my father emigrated, he first lived with Uncle Carl and Aunt Christine and Cousin Paul. Carl was his official sponsor. When Carl decided to move to the North Side of Chicago and begin his general contracting business there, my father decided to stay on the South Side to help Ephraim in his contracting business.

Carl seemed to be more of a risk-taker than the other two brothers. For example, he bought property in Florida in the 1930s on speculation, which he ultimately lost.

He joined the Ravenswood Covenant Church on the North Side, whereas David and Ephraim were active members of Bethany Covenant Church on the South Side. Carl was a very involved member. One Monday morning when he had volunteered to help clean the church basement, he suffered a fatal heart attack and died at the age of only fifty-one.

Because Paul had marvelous powers of concentration and a memory like a steel trap, he managed to complete law studies at night at Chicago Kent College of Law, while working as a runner in a law office during the day and also working in the library at North Park College.

After his father's death in the fall, Paul followed the classified ads to find employment in a law office to support his mother and himself. After answering an ad and being interviewed, he made the decision to go into his own practice. He told the interviewer he would take his chances on making it on his own rather than work for someone else at the low salary offered. He never did work for anyone else.

The loss of his father played a very significant part in shaping Paul's life, for Carl left his wife and son in a bankrupt condition. I think this situation laid the groundwork for Paul's business and professional success. I recall Paul reassuring his mother that as long as he was alive, she would never have to worry about anything and he would always take care of her.

No doubt the seeds of the retirement centers of The Evangelical Covenant Church were planted at this time. When Paul married Vega Rundquist in 1938, he tried everything in his search to find good housing accommodations for his mother. She lived with them for a while, and she also lived with other people and with me.

Paul had a soft spot in his heart for older people. He saw the plight of his mother multiplied many times over. His burgeoning law practice in estates was a constant reminder of the pressing need for a good life after one spouse dies. He began to devote considerable energy to fulfilling a dream.

He was elected to the Covenant Board of Benevolence and exercised his influence to expand its horizons and create retirement communities throughout the United States. He was a visionary. Sometimes it was difficult for others to embrace his ideas as quickly as he would have liked. But he also had the patience of Job. He was philosophical; if others could not go along at the pace he set, he would try to accommodate them even as his mind raced on to other ideas.

His mind worked like a computer, with fantastic recall, and woe unto anyone who would try to trick him. I know, for I learned to play Monopoly with Paul at his family's kitchen table on North Hermitage Avenue. Every summer I was invited to stay with Aunt Christine. I so looked forward to this, for I especially enjoyed spending time with my big cousin, Paul. Although he was going to school full time and working, he always found time to play Monopoly with me. I adored him. As I look back, I wonder if he thought of me as a big pain, but he never acted that way.

We both loved books and were insatiable readers with wide interests. Paul was not very athletic, but he could play a wicked game of table tennis. I tried unsuccessfully time and again to beat him, but he was unbeatable. When he tackled something, whether table tennis, chess, or any parlor game, he played to win. His power of concentration served him in good stead in whatever he undertook.

When Paul married Vega, I was twelve years old. I cried uncontrollably at the wedding. She used to tease me that I didn't like her, but that wasn't the case at all. Somehow I just knew that from now on things would be different, that Paul wouldn't be able to share his time like he used to do. After I matured a bit, we all became close at a different level. When their daughter, Carola, was born, I was fifteen. We have shared a close relationship similar to the one Paul and I had.

My high school graduation stands out in memory, for I was to be the piano soloist and wanted so much for Paul to be there. My parents discouraged my inviting him because of his busy schedule, but I did and he came. I was ecstatic. I later noticed how Paul always made time to attend the traditional rituals of weddings, funerals, and graduations of any of his friends or their children. He was very loyal and gave of his time freely.

He loved to sing and could remember all the stanzas of his favorite hymns. Sometimes he'd break out in Swedish, singing lustily, enjoying the reactions of others, and challenging them to join in.

As he became financially more secure, and I'm not sure the phrase applies, for he was a tremendous risk-taker, he had the equanimity to take gambles most people wouldn't make. He used to tell me it was all a game and that he came into this world with nothing and he was going to leave the same way, but in the meantime he was going to follow his vision and if things worked out—"terrriffficcc" (I can still hear him drawing out that word with a lilt in his voice). And if they didn't? He'd shrug his shoulders and roll his eyes. He truly enjoyed the process and the challenge of every day.

Challenge seemed to be a byword with Paul. Over and over, he would challenge organizations and individuals to match his giving. In order for him to keep his side of the bargain, he sometimes had to borrow the money. I know he made people squirm with his challenges, but he believed strongly that "the more you give, the more you will receive," and he exemplified this himself. He believed that the Lord loveth a cheerful giver, and he lived this also.

He loved helping young people, especially in their education. The actual numbers I do not know, but they were countless. My two stepdaughters, Kathy and Barbie, benefitted. Kathy enjoyed one year at North Park College, and Barbie went all four years. This was a positive interlude in their lives. When I undertook a doctoral program at the University of Southern California, Paul was there to encourage me and help financially, if needed.

He was always available for consultation, whether it was personal or financial. He gave of himself—unsparingly. He was willing to help people fulfill their dreams, thereby encouraging them to do the same for others. I remember that he was so busy helping others get their income tax done on time that he had to drive downtown Chicago to put his own return in the mailbox at the very last minute.

During Carola's freshman year at North Park Academy, Paul asked me to come and live with them since Vega was not feeling well. I was happy to do this, for I enjoyed the company of all of them, and it was fun to act as Carola's big sister. We did a lot of things together. I loved camping, and Carola was game for any adventure.

When I accepted a position at California State University at Long Beach, Carola and my friend, Jean Carlin, joined me as we camped from Minneapolis to Salt Lake City. Especially do I enjoy the memory of Carola's sixteenth birthday, waking up to a soft snowfall on our faces as we were sleeping outside in our down sleeping bags at Jenny Lake in the Grand Tetons. Paul loved to tell the stories about his girls and their adventures—he had a vicarious enjoyment of our trips.

On another vacation we were deep-sea fishing off the Florida coast. I hooked a dolphin, and Paul was so excited. He wanted me to reel it in so it could be stuffed, but I didn't like the idea and let it go. He expressed his annoyance with me in no uncertain terms.

He loved to bait me on political issues, which would drive me deeper into taking the opposite viewpoint. He had the annoying habit of wanting to be right, and so did I. He seldom called a truce (others did it for us), but secretly we both enjoyed the sparring. He loved matching wits with anyone, and he liked to intimidate. I knew him too well to be intimidated, but I was still in awe of him and of his ability to visualize a concept and then set it into motion.

The Covenant Retirement Communities are the primary dream that comes to mind. He was so determined that his mother would live out her life as comfortably and with as much dignity as possible. He believed strongly that couples should go in together, so that if one dies suddenly the remaining partner has less of an adjustment as well as a built-in support system. He thought the idea of living in a retirement community so good that he was one of the first to buy a duplex at Covenant Village of Northbrook.

Vega didn't live long enough to move into Northbrook. She died of a ruptured aneurysm in 1970, and this was a shock to all of us. The great lesson I learned from her death was to see how Paul reacted. He shared with me how important it is to let people know while they are alive how much they mean to you so that you can go on living with minimal regrets. He did everything he could to please her, and she did her best to be the perfect hostess and wife.

After her funeral, he asked me to fly down to Florida with him to visit his mother, who was now living comfortably at Covenant Palms of Miami. On the plane, he talked about his life with Vega. Her stress-related health problems piqued his interest in mental health, and consequently he co-founded, along with W. Clement Stone, the Stone-Brandel Center (for mental health) in Chicago. I thought to myself, how interesting that both his mother and his wife played such important roles in determining the direction of Paul's energies and money.

There was another woman in his life who played a very important part, and that was his lifelong friend, secretary, and subsequently, second wife, Bernice. Bernice was married to Henry Stege, and they had the other half of the duplex in Northbrook. Vega and Paul and Bernice and Henry were childhood friends from Ravenswood Covenant Church.

When Paul's law practice needed a full-time secretary, he asked Bernice to join him and help organize the office. She became indispensable. She came to know as much about the business as he. She also served on the Covenant Board of Benevolence. The two were an unbeatable team.

After Henry died, Paul and Bernice married in 1976. They were happily married for nearly eleven years. They used to celebrate their wedding anniversary by the month rather than the year, for they felt they didn't have too much time. I think that these were some of the happiest years of Paul's life, for he traveled widely, was able to realize the fruits of his labors, and was in a comfortable position. Bernice was the ideal companion, still serving as Paul's secretary but adding on the roles of hostess and wife. They had an enviable life together, marred only by Paul's failing health. He taught her well his philosophy of stewardship, and she is continuing his legacy of giving so that many people's lives are further enriched.

My beloved father is living out his remaining years in the Brandel

Care Center at Northbrook. He loves to sit in his wheelchair and look at Paul's portrait hanging by the entrance and just talk to him. I think we all do this when we pass his portrait.

I'm thankful for the legacy Paul has given us and the challenge he has left to give generously of ourselves and our means. No matter what the size of our largesse, the important thing is to share what we have—willingly and cheerfully.

THE POOREST RICH MAN

W. CLEMENT STONE

*W. Clement Stone is widely known for his
PMA (positive mental attitude) philosophy and
as an insurance executive—chairman emeritus
of Aon Corporation—philanthropist, civic leader,
author, and publisher.*

O f all the people I have met in my business career, I can think of only a few I would submit without hesitation as candidates for sainthood. Undoubtedly, the name of Paul Brandel would be foremost among them.

Paul and I were associated from 1965 until his death in 1986, and never once during those twenty-one years did I hear him utter an unkind word about another person or suggest any action in our real-estate dealings that might take unfair advantage of someone or be in the slightest degree unethical. He was a model of Christian charity and stewardship, giving freely of his time, talent, and treasure to worthy causes.

It was in this role that Paul and I first met in the office of my home in Evanston, from which I conducted much of my business. He arrived accompanied by his secretary, Bernice, who was to record the meeting. I had called in my own secretary, Minnie Clark, and my principal advisor, the late Sen. Russell Arrington, because although I was not sure exactly what my visitor was going to propose, I knew from a memo I'd received through Bill Neverman, vice-president of investments of my company, Combined Insurance Company of America, that Mr. Brandel had in mind a very large real-estate investment.

I liked Paul immediately. He had a twinkle in his eye that appealed to me, and I found both the magnitude of his proposal and its purpose captivating.

Paul had learned from his real-estate associate, Andy Sakelson, that St. Luke's Hospital was about to vacate its buildings at 14th and Michigan Avenue, on the Near South Side of Chicago, and would be merging with Presbyterian Hospital. Paul's hope was to buy the St. Luke's property and turn it into a hospital, nursing home, and retirement center.

He told us the story of Swedish Covenant Hospital, how it had developed out of the Home of Mercy, which after the turn of the century had served Chicago's Swedish immigrant community as an orphanage, old people's home, and shelter for the poor and needy. He explained how, through his position as a leader in The Evangelical Covenant Church, he had helped develop Covenant Palms of Miami, a continuing-care home for the elderly that was the first of a projected nationwide development of Covenant Retirement Communities.

From there he went on to describe his dream for the St. Luke's property, and I must say that, in his understated way, he painted an appealing picture.

The amount of money required for the purchase of St. Luke's was significant, and Russ Arrington raised a number of objections to such an investment on my part with its possible tax implications. We concluded the meeting with an agreement to get together the following week. I then asked Russ to check into Paul's financial status and report to me prior to that session.

A few days later, I met with Russ and my financial advisor, Ken Danielson. I said, "Well, what do you think?" Ken replied, "I have obtained an audited statement from Mr. Brandel that shows he is worth $10 million." That, I told them, was good enough for me.

I was excited by Paul's idea. I thought its vision of rendering medical service in a humanitarian context was wonderful. Moreover, I was extremely interested in mental health, having just completed writing my book *The Other Side of the Mind* with Norma Lee Browning, and I could see possibilities in Paul's idea for opening a unique mental-health facility.

The result of our combined efforts was the Stone-Brandel Center, which opened in 1966. It had a full-time staff directed by Wallace Buya, and Dr. Karl Menninger was in residence as our senior consultant. There were also eight or more affiliated organizations that used the center's facilities, including the Illinois branch of the American Foundation of Religion and Psychiatry, whose parent organization was established by my friends Dr. Norman Vincent Peale and Smiley Blanton; the Warren Clinic, which provided diagnostic and treatment services to alcoholics and their families; the Dyslexia Memorial Institute; and Bearings, Inc., which provided job counseling for former clergy and religious communities of all faiths.

The center's own programs were diverse. They included suicide and crisis intervention, achievement and motivation programs, a pre-release education program for state and federal prisoners, the Katherine Wright Mental Health Clinic, and the Youth Mental Health Project in cooperation with the Chicago Boys Clubs.

Paul and I would attend the executive board meetings, and they sometimes became highly emotional when the program directors were hashing out conflicting views on policy or pleading for funding for some new project. But Paul was imperturbable. Without raising his voice, he would explain what the facts were and how they should be considered for the benefit of the organization and the people it was meant to serve. This usually restored calm and order.

"You remind me of your namesake, St. Paul," I told him after one such session. He cocked a quizzical eyebrow at me, and I explained, "Paul says in 2 Corinthians, 'When I am weak, you are strong.' "

"No Clem," he said. "I love Christ, but I have not Paul's inspired zeal. Nor do I strive to be all things to all men."

Nonetheless, there was great strength under Paul's quiet, self-effacing manner, as I saw illustrated on many occasions. Once, for example, Wally Buya came to us with a vexing personnel problem. Certain staffers were making salary demands that were out of line with our budget. Paul suggested to Wally that he tell them the money simply wasn't available and they would have to be content with their present salaries.

"But what if they won't accept that?" Wally asked.

Paul pointed toward the main entrance and said, "Just tell them that door swings both ways."

The Stone-Brandel Center was reorganized after about three years and its activities were transferred to other auspices. But by then Paul and I were involved in many other things together.

One of our areas of mutual interest was real-estate investment.

Paul had a true genius for selecting property that would grow and appreciate. For example, he bought some land in the countryside northwest of Chicago that seemed good for nothing but growing corn. Gradually communities sprang up in the area, and eventually the property was developed by some shopping-center builders. It is now Woodfield Mall, located in one of the country's fastest growing residential areas.

Paul's vision was highly creative. He came to me one day with an idea for purchasing air rights over the Illinois Central railroad tracks in downtown Chicago and building a skyscraper that would be taller than the Empire State Building.

"Wow, this is a terrific idea!" I told him. We were like a couple of boys building a clubhouse, excitedly topping each other's plans for more magnificent features.

Unfortunately, we were about twenty years ahead of the time when building on air rights would be widely accepted, and legal complications kept our pie-in-the-sky plan from materializing. But it sure was fun while it lasted. Incidentally, a plan was announced recently for a major office and condominium development using those same air rights.

Another situation Paul and I got involved in was a 146-acre farm near Barrington, Illinois. It was owned by an old-timer named Robert Westphalen, who had worked the land all his life and was the last of his clan in the area. He had contacted Paul early in 1973, because he was told by someone he trusted that Paul was an honest man who would help him sell his farm in such a way that all the money would go to charity. I was interested in acquiring the property because it abutted another farm of fifty acres called Hidden Brook, which I had purchased in 1964.

The arrangement Paul and I worked out was for me to purchase the farm for $1 million. The payments would be $100,000 annually for ten years, and each year I would write a check in that amount to one of the charities Mr. Westphalen named. He was a Catholic, and it was not surprising that several Catholic charities were among them, but so was the Salvation Army.

Mr. Westphalen was about ninety years old when I met him. He was dressed in worn, ill-fitting clothes and looked like he could have used a handout. Yet he was giving everything he had to charity. It was very touching, and Paul was most solicitous toward him.

One day Paul told me he had received a call from Mr. Westphalen's neighbor, who was concerned because he had not seen the old man out and about. "I went there to check up on him," Paul said, "and he was just sitting in a rocking chair staring into space. At first I thought he was dead, but he was just in kind of a trance. He told me he didn't feel like going outside, didn't feel like fixing himself anything to eat, and couldn't find things around the house.

"I took care of him the best I could. I wish I could get him to come to Swedish Covenant Hospital, but he won't hear of it. He doesn't want to leave that house."

Mr. Westphalen died not long after that, and a will was found in which he asked that Paul Brandel take care of his burial in a cemetery somewhere in Iowa. Paul arranged for a funeral in the Catholic church in Barrington. Mr. Westphalen didn't have a suit to be buried in, so Paul bought one. Then Paul set out to find the cemetery referred to. As I recall, the only clue he had was that Mr. Westphalen had a brother who was buried in that place. After many phone calls to undertakers in that part of Iowa, he found the cemetery and took the body there to be buried. All of those expenses came out of Paul's own pocket, and I doubt that anyone but his wife and I knew about this particular act of Christian charity.

This episode points to a characteristic of Paul's generous spirit that I always admired—he seldom took credit for his good deeds. He preferred to remain anonymous. He allowed us to put his name on the Stone-Brandel Center, but he never wanted credit in press releases or other publicity for the wonderful programs he helped initiate.

I was Paul's opposite in that respect. I believe in the value of publicity and showmanship, not to gratify my own ego but to build interest and value in the projects with which I am associated.

Sometimes I thought Paul carried his humility too far, and I would urge him to take some of the limelight that was falling on me. He'd say, "No, Clem, you're the one who knows how to dazzle a crowd. I'm more comfortable looking on from the wings."

Before I get too far from the story of Paul and Mr. Westphalen, I want to mention an interesting twist that occurred with that property. In 1986, I joined with Jack Nicklaus, the famous golfer and golf-course designer, to build a golf course surrounded by luxury residences on the Westphalen land, along with Hidden Brook and another 176 acres on which I had options. The development is called Wynstone, and I think Paul would applaud this outcome.

I don't want to convey the impression that Paul wasn't interested in making money. He was, and he was extremely good at it. I recall one option he picked up on four corners in what is now Buffalo Grove for $5,000. He made some further payments in order to keep the options, and some people thought he was going to lose money on the thing. Then a developer came along with a plan for which those four corners were vital, and he paid Paul $500,000 for his option.

You might be able to guess what Paul did with the money. He put most of it into a trust for Covenant Retirement Communities.

Another reason I respected Paul was for his willingness to serve on the boards of various organizations in which I was interested. One was the International Council for the Education of Teachers. ICET had perpetual funding problems, and I was called on from time to time to bail it out of a jam. On one occasion, I met with Paul and another board member, Robert Neuschel, a former vice-president of McKenzie & Company who had retired to teach in Northwestern University's Kellogg Graduate School of Management.

I opened the meeting by outlining how much ICET needed and how much I was prepared to give, but Paul broke in and said, "Clem, giving them the money is not the right thing to do. This organization needs to become self-sufficient." Then with that wonderful way he had with parables or wise sayings to make a point, he said, "If you give them a fish, you will feed them for a day. If you teach them to fish, you will feed them for a lifetime."

After that Paul served as something of a whistle-blower on the ICET board. Whenever members began asking for alms instead of working harder at fundraising, Paul would give one of his gentle cowhiding speeches that would cut deep without raising a welt, and the board would wonder how it ever came up with such a silly idea in the first place. Despite his firm position on funding discipline, Paul was one of the few individuals besides me who made monetary contributions to the organization.

The ICET board was special, because ICET meets in a different country each year, and this gave Paul and his wife many opportunities to travel together with my wife, Jessie, and me.

It was a joy to travel with Paul, because he had such a sense of historical perspective and could make an ordinary tourist-stroll through a church or marketplace into a rich experience. I recall one trip to Rome when Paul and Bob Neuschel took us on a verbal exploration of early Christianity as we toured St. Peter's and the Roman ruins.

Paul was always eloquent in saying grace, which he did before every meal. But during that trip to Rome he seemed inspired. His blessings were extemporaneous, crafted to suit the particular place in which we happened to be dining, and were adorned with gemlike turns of phrase. One evening we had dinner at the Hassler Hotel, also known as the Villa de Medici, at the top of the Spanish Steps. The view of the city spread out below us was magnificent, and Paul used the phrase "close to heaven" in asking the blessing. That's all I can remember of that prayer, but it captured a feeling each of us had at the moment.

I don't think I ever talked politics with Paul Brandel. I am not even sure what his party affiliation was, but I would imagine it was conservative Republican. I know that despite his willingness to take what seemed to be big risks in real estate, he was very conservative.

For example, when we were getting started at the Stone-Brandel Center, Dr. Menninger outlined to the board a very ambitious mental-health plan that called for doubling the psychiatric staff and the scope of its services in six months. Wally Buya remembers that after the meeting Paul approached him and said, "This plan that was being discussed in the board meeting is going to cost too much money, and I want you to know that I am not going to be in a position to support it."

"I told him I would mention that to Mr. Stone," Wally continues, "and Paul said, 'Mr. Stone isn't going to fund it either. It is going to cost more than a million dollars.'

" 'Well,' I said, 'that's what our current thinking is,' and Paul added, 'You aren't going to be able to see Mr. Stone anyhow. He and his wife are on their way to Europe, they'll be gone three or four weeks, and Dr. Karl wants to start this program immediately.' "

In fact, Wally did catch me at O'Hare Airport, just before Jessie and I got on the plane. He explained the situation, and I approved the expenditure. When Paul learned about my decision he went along with it, but the incident demonstrates that he was much more cautious and conservative in such things than I was.

Paul was wealthy, but his investments were not the kind that generated much cash flow. Linda Rupp, who has been my assistant for more than a dozen years and who worked closely with me in my dealings with Paul, once observed that he was the poorest rich man she knew. Which was true, for Paul embodied the spirit of Euripides's lines:

> I care for riches to make gifts
> To friends, or lead a sick man back to health
> With ease and plenty. Else small aid is wealth
> For daily gladness; once a man be done
> With hunger, rich and poor are all as one.

Paul lived his faith completely. To my knowledge he never played cards or danced or drank alcohol. I, on the other hand, love to play bridge, enjoy ballroom dancing, and think there are few pleasures in life finer than a good cigar and a glass of champagne after dinner. Paul never criticized, although I suppose he might have if my worldly habits had been less moderate.

Come to think of it, Wally Buya once told me that he was present on an occasion when Paul drank some wine. They were flying back to the United States from a conference Dr. Menninger had arranged in England. Wally ordered some wine from the flight attendant at dinner, and Paul told her he thought he would take a glass, too. Wally was astounded; perhaps it had something to do with the fact that they had just spent a week in the midst of 2,000 psychiatrists.

Paul did not go in for material possessions or for making a display of wealth. He did have a beautiful farm at Williams Bay, Wisconsin, where he raised Arabian horses and Black Angus cattle, but that somehow seemed more an extension of his stewardship role than pleasure-seeking.

Each year he would invite his friends and all the residents from Covenant Village of Northbrook to his farm for a huge picnic. It was an event we all looked forward to, and one year my son Clem had an experience up there that I'll always remember.

Clem had just returned from England, where he had been in charge of our Combined International operations. He knew Paul only slightly, and he had never been to the farm. When he and his wife drove up there the day of the picnic, they couldn't find the place. He stopped in a local tavern and asked the bartender, who shouted, "Brandel farm? Nope. Any you fellas know a Brandel place?" None of the patrons showed a flicker of recognition. Clem stopped at a gas station, no soap. Then he pulled up to a grocery store, same story.

Finally, after more aimless driving about, Clem stopped at a church, where a lady said, "Oh certainly, we know Mr. Brandel," and she showed him the way. Clem never got over that. He'd say, "If you want to find Paul Brandel, just go to church."

I found, in thinking about my relationship with Paul for this reminiscence, that Clem's observation is still true.

At first I had a problem remembering details of some of the incidents I wanted to set down in these pages. Then, during Sunday services at our Presbyterian church in Evanston, I looked up at the cross of gold above the altar, and the memories of Paul and his stewardship came flooding back!

Serving the Church with Uniqueness and Expertise

MILTON B. ENGEBRETSON

Milton B. Engebretson served as president of The Evangelical Covenant Church for nineteen years and is now president emeritus and minister-at-large.

D octor, lawyer, merchant, chief." Paul Brandel could have responded in a roll call to any of the above, plus counselor, fiduciary, entrepreneur, manager, administrator, salesman, promoter, philanthropist, planner, speaker; the list goes on. He was about as versatile as they come.

In some things cerebral, he bordered on brilliance. Physical was another matter. His father at one time had thoughts of developing a tradesman out of him and took him along at about age fifteen to teach him the skill of carpentry. He put a hammer in his hand, attempted to teach him how to use it, gave him an ample supply of nails, and went off to do his own work. It was the simplest form of nailing possible—tacking plywood to joists to build a floor. No toe-nailing, overhead, tight-corner, or mitre work. Something almost anyone could do, anyone except Paul, that is.

A couple of hours after giving the assignment, the senior Brandel returned. The results were disastrous. He quickly reached the only sane conclusion possible and said, "I can see this is hopeless, son; you better go on to more schooling where you can learn to do something with your mind. It's for sure you'll never make it with your hands."

And so it was on to college and from there to law school. Paul's father made a wise decision and one that enabled Paul to fulfill the deepest aspirations residual in that bright mind of his and prepared him to serve Christ and the church with a uniqueness and expertise more crucial to the Covenant's future than many people know.

He was a fascinating combination of genes and chromosomes. He loved loyalty, brevity, philanthropy, generosity, faith, unity, humor, traditional values, freewheeling speech, short sermons, solving problems, attempting the impossible, directing operations, and being Republican. He disliked fads, clergy dominance, bureaucracy, labor unions, long sermons or even long meetings, bearded faces, and the Democratic Party. This spate of preferences and qualities made him the kind of person he came to be and enabled him to accomplish what he did.

His long suit, of course, was stewardship. He understood money, financial planning, and values. He was also skilled in relating these to faith and commitment. There was very little difference between his pronouncements and his practice. He was one of those rare persons who could say, while talking about Christian philanthropy, "Do as I do, and God will always get his share of what you earn." One has to wonder where this unusual sense of stewardship came from.

We tend to discredit the incredible potential pastors have for influencing impressionable minds during their formative years. Pastors can either exert such influence or completely miss it by how they live and what they teach. Most of us admit we were somewhat redirected by the example and witness of certain individuals, but seldom do we hear of life-changing practices adopted by people because of the ministries of certain pastors.

With Paul it was different. He often commented on the good fortune that was his to be led and taught by the pastor of his youth. It changed the whole pattern of his life. August J. Almquist served the Ravenswood Covenant Church in Chicago from 1917 to 1933. Paul attended Ravenswood from his childhood through his thirties, except for a year his family spent in Florida when he was in high school. Pastor Almquist began that ministry at age fifty. He was highly regarded by Paul, and others who were members during the Almquist years have filled me in on his effective influence on the parishioners. Paul told me twenty times if he told me once that Almquist taught him proportionate giving as both the obligation and privilege of a Christian so convincingly that it became the modus operandi for the management of his life. Paul concluded almost every speech he ever gave with a line learned from the pastor of his youth, "Keep on giving to God until God stops giving to you."

Almquist preached one stewardship sermon every month, and if there were five Sundays he preached two. The first principle he stressed was that God is a God of abundance who will always be faithful to you. The second truth indelibly inscribed in Paul's mind was that faith is the basis for giving. "You do not pledge your giving for the coming year on the basis of what you earned last year or even on your current assets," he always said, "but on the increases in income and investments that you can reasonably expect God to bless you with during the coming year."

If one were at all industrious in the period of economic expansion in which Paul lived, both income and assets would surely increase with each year of employment or business ownership. Therefore, all pledges made to God and his church should be made in faith on what you expect to receive. What Paul currently owned and managed was to be used simply as a base to calculate the size of the contribution under consideration. If one's holdings were large, the gifts could be anticipated to be larger. His own risk taking was at times scary, but, to my knowledge, he never welshed on a promise.

These convictions were so deeply ingrained in his thinking that I don't think he ever conceptualized anything as being his alone. Any gain, any unanticipated rise in prosperity, any good fortune that came his way, was always figured in terms of how this would enable him to give more to the church of Jesus Christ and other needy causes. He was one of the few persons with whom I worked closely who was always planning new ways to give more. It seemed as if he was captivated by the necessity to give. In the words of Lloyd Douglas, it was a kind of "magnificent obsession." To me, it was simply incredible.

Paul loved to speak on Christian stewardship. It mattered little what the occasion was or the topic assigned, Paul spoke on stewardship.

In 1972 he was invited to give the commencement address at the College of Emporia in Kansas, where he was being honored with a doctor of literature and letters degree. When he returned, somewhat pleased with his performance, I asked, "What did you speak about, Paul?" He responded, "What do you think, the same as I have spoken every place I've been for the past ten years—time, talent, and treasure." There was little variation from speech to speech. He always spoke from the script written in his brain, never from an outline or manuscript. "Those only enslave and confuse me," he would say.

We traveled together for year-end fundraising events every year for the six years he was chairman of the Covenant Trustees. Aside from updating facts and data, his speech was essentially the same in year six as it was in year one. His four points were: The first twenty years you belong to Mama. The second twenty years, you're learning something. The third twenty years, you're earning something. And the fourth twenty years, you had better start finding ways to give away most of what you have earned and get ready to meet the one who gave you the ability to earn and amass what you have.

The last point was considerably longer than the other three points. Actually this was part of his methodical consistency, too, because he rarely mentioned points one and two after stating them. To him they were only steppingstones to the final act on the grand stage where life would determine who, after all, had the supreme allegiance in one's thoughts and actions. Paul believed that if, as a Christian, "whatever your heart clings to and confides in" (Martin Luther) is the God and Father of the Lord Jesus Christ, it follows like night follows day that it will always be God who profits most from whatever material gain comes—a principle that to me is both biblically defensible and commendable.

Paul gave a little attention to point three, because he felt that he needed to articulate God's part in a person's earnings. Paul believed and taught that proportionate giving is every person's reciprocal responsibility to God's goodness, and it all begins with the first dollar owned or the first assets acquired and continues throughout the entirety of life.

On occasion, I would tell Paul that I had a lunch scheduled with someone who had recently come into wealth, for the purpose of challenging this person to give a sizable gift to the Covenant. Paul would say, "Save your breath to blow on your soup. This person did not give when he had little, so it is very unlikely he will give now that he has much." The strange thing is that this axiom, if it can be so-called, has proven to be true in case after case.

Paul loved passages like Deuteronomy 8:11-14 and 18 (TEV): "Make certain that you do not forget the Lord your God; do not fail to obey any of his laws that I am giving you today. When you have all you want to eat and have built good houses to live in and when your cattle and sheep, your silver and gold, and all your other possessions have increased, be sure that you do not become proud and forget the Lord your God. . . . Remember that it is the Lord your God who gives you the power to become rich. He does this because he is still faithful today to the covenant that he made with your ancestors."

Perhaps the reason for Paul's preoccupation with point number four was that he was in the last twenty-year period of his life during the time we worked together. His mind was filled with both systems and methods for giving. He encouraged me to take the step in 1978 to create an office of planned giving for the Covenant. This meant the removal of all responsibility for planned giving from the office of stewardship. It also called for the coordination of the estate planning offices of North Park College and Theological Seminary, Swedish Covenant Hospital, and the Board of Benevolence, placing all under one administrator.

It was a masterful stroke, and with LeRoy M. Johnson appointed to be executive director, the progress reads almost like a Lee Iacocca success story. Recently the Covenant Trust Company was formed, which complies with regulations and standards imposed by the Illinois Commissioner of Banks and Trust Companies. There is no denomination the size of the Covenant that has anything even approximating what has been accomplished by this move, and it all happened in ten short years. The future possibilities for this venture for the Covenant, its institutions, its regional conferences, and its local churches are enormous. I seriously doubt that it would ever have happened without the inspiration and encouragement of Paul Brandel.

It was Paul's vision for the church that made him such a dynamic force among us—his vision for the best in hospital care and the best for senior adults during their retirement years. This may sound as if the venture of building and maintaining retirement centers was a solo flight by Paul. It was also the successful operation it is today because of Nils G. Axelson. In fact, the unique combination of Paul and Nils can be largely credited for the success of the entire benevolence operation.

There were others also, good administrators such as Harry Ekstam, James Aspegren, Paul V. Peterson, and James Drevets, plus board members such as Donald Michealsen and Rolland Carlson, et al.

Paul also would not have been the person I have attempted to describe without Bernice, his able secretary and administrative assistant for thirty years and his spouse for the last eleven years of his life. She not only kept order in the chaos of his multifaceted operation, but she continually bolstered his spirits and always inspired him to do his best.

There was one distinguishing characteristic of Paul that set him apart from most philanthropists, and that was the dimension of hope that he was somehow capable of infusing into every situation. When a committee had all of its plans in order but couldn't proceed any further for lack of financial resources, then the person who planted the seeds for the project in the first place would say, "Well, go ahead, give it your best shot, and if you can't make it, I'll make up the difference." That breeds hope. This Paul did time after time after time. Consequently, committees with that kind of backing gave it a go and usually made the goal without ever calling upon the reinforcements offered. There were exceptions, however, and then the promised resources were given.

One might think Paul's stewardship sermon was a nice bit of rhetoric, something to stir people to action. That could be the case for a person of average financial holdings but not for a person with the financial base commanded by Paul Brandel. It was a fairly gutsy pronouncement on which he was always prepared to make good. To my knowledge, he did everything possible to give away most of what he had during the last twenty years of his life. Had he lived longer, he would have given more.

I first met Paul the day I was elected to the office of secretary of the Covenant. It was June 1962, during the Covenant Annual Meeting on the campus of Seattle Pacific College, now Seattle Pacific University. It was during the missionary banquet, held in the athletic complex. It was a long meeting and probably one of the hottest and most uncomfortable I have every attempted to endure. The catering staff was over its head in its struggle to serve the meal in a place that was grossly overcrowded. We finally received our food but never anything to drink. At long last, I decided to try to make it outside to get some water or cola to slake the parched throats of my friends and me. After what seemed like a half-hour trip, stumbling over people and disturbing the uneven flow of the speakers, who weren't being listened to anyway, I finally reached the exit. Once I got out, there was no returning.

About a hundred paces from the door, I met the man who carried the name I had heard so often but so far had neither seen nor met—Paul W. Brandel, esq. He was there with his pastor, Clifford W. Bjorklund, who was wearing a surgical collar due to a recent whiplash from an auto accident, and of course Nils G. Axelson. About a minute and a half past introductions, I was exposed to what I later came to recognize as a typical Brandelian tirade against long meetings and long sermons. About two minutes later, since I had just been elected as a new Covenant administrator, he began preaching to me about PMA with OPM—positive mental attitude with other people's money. It was refreshing.

This meeting was one of those rare indelible moments that permanently inscribe itself in one's memory. Little did I realize that the instant kinship I felt at that meeting would grow into a friendship that would link us together in the leadership of the church for the rest of his life and through my tenure as an administrator.

Later on, as we worked together, I began to see the pattern that governed his life. There were three distinguishing emphases that characterized his view of property, money, and ownership, which composed his philosophy and theology of a Christian's managerial responsibilities before God and humankind.

First, it was rarely anything but positive. He approached a situation from a position of possibility. His oft-repeated phrase was, "I think it is do-able." If, however, he didn't approve of the proposal being considered, he came down just as strongly against it. In fact, it was difficult for him to see how anyone could propose, much less support, anything contrary to his irrefutable logic. Paul's margin for the in-between was fairly thin. He was not overly endowed with patience for those whose viewpoints differed from his. He somehow just naturally expected both concurrence and support after he had taken the pains to explain the fantastic potential for benefits, if done according to his unquestionably superior plan. He was progress-oriented, not problem-centered. He always tried his best to get others to be the same, and he had a pretty good record of success.

Second, he believed in helping people help themselves. Several times, people in a specific locale became interested in having the

Covenant build a retirement center. Paul's response was always negative unless they were willing to extend themselves, get involved, generate the funds to build the first unit, construct it, operate it, and achieve 100 percent occupancy. Then if they were still interested, the Board of Benevolence would be glad to assume ownership and develop it to the limits of its potential. This ensured that the board would be building a center with them, not for them.

One example of his convictions about this was a time when he was invited to speak at a men's retreat at a Covenant camp. Upon arrival, it was obvious that the board and conference were involved in adding new buildings to meet the needs for a larger camp and to improve the quality of the place. Paul liked what he saw, so in his first address he, very characteristically, threw out a challenge.

"Here is your chance," said he, "to make a great stride forward in funding your building program. Every dollar that is given this weekend, while I am with you, I will match with another dollar." When he returned to Chicago, the wheels of the plane had barely touched the runway before he was on the phone to tell me what happened. "Milt, I can't believe those guys. I offered to match anything they would give for that camp; I sincerely prepared myself to give $50,000. Do you know what they gave? The total amount was less than $200." They may have misunderstood his intentions or the challenge. The truth is that by their giving they could have picked up enough from the challenge alone to finance one of those beautiful buildings.

Third, Paul assumed personal financial responsibility for whatever he was a part of. He served as the chairman of fundraising drives for the Red Cross, the Salvation Army, Goodwill Industries, several colleges, and numerous other organizations. In true biblical fashion, he put his own life on the line first. He made responsibility for the success of the operation a personal thing.

When we were planning the Giving for Growing Campaign in 1974, the outlook seemed a little bleak to me. Inflation was rising, unemployment was pushing higher, and the tick was negative on the Dow Jones averages almost every day. It was scary. Paul, Ralph Hanson (campaign executive director), and I were eating dinner at a restaurant in Wheeling, Illinois, and I began to share my concerns. We were just starting to contact major donors to attempt to get the first $3,000,000 of the $7,500,000 goal.

Paul's response was, "What are you worried about, you've already got your first million." After I caught my breath, I said, "Wow! Then that means we already have two million, because A. Harold and Lorraine Anderson are pledging the same." As it turned out, about thirty other Covenanters gave major amounts, which brought total major gifts to $3,000,000. With this amount assured, our churches came through and overshot the goal, pledging almost $5,000,000, bringing the total close to $8,000,000.

The 1970s were lean years financially for the Covenant while Paul was chairman of the Trustees. We closed a few fiscal years with losses that gradually reached an operating deficit of about $300,000. We chipped away and reduced it to $277,000, and that's where it was when Paul was about to complete his term in 1977. In the spring of that year, he called me one day and asked if I could stop by his office. I returned to the Covenant Office from that trip elated, with a check for $245,000 in my pocket that Paul gave to bring the deficit to a wash before he completed his term. This was in addition to his yearly contributions to the budget, which were not small. He was one of the few wealthy people I have met who always made his own gift first, and one who was constantly looking for causes worthy of what he considered to be the Lord's money entrusted to his management. He was very generous—and almost unbelievable.

Aside from stewardship concerns, we did many things together. On one occasion I was invited to Yakutat, Alaska, and given the trip by the Bureau of Indian Affairs for the purpose of our granting a lease of about twenty-five acres of land for low-income housing for the Indians residing there. It seemed only right, particularly since the trip was paid for, to invite the chairman of the Trustees along. After our meeting discussing the lease, I arranged for a day's sightseeing trip on two private planes with John and Eleanor Claus.

We flew out of Anchorage off the very limited landing strip in the Clauses' backyard in two Piper SuperCub airplanes, each capable of transporting one pilot and one passenger. We flew across the corner of Elmendorf Air Force Base and over the narrow part of Cook Inlet with a view of Mount Susitna and the Talkeetna Mountains, across the hunting grounds in the Matanuska Valley, and on past the oil wells in the inlet with their helicopter landing platforms. We were always in sight of that glorious Alaskan Range, displaying the beauty of Mount Foraker and Mount Dall with Mount McKinley rising majestically above the others to its 20,232-foot height in the background. All were brightly clothed in the pure white snows of winter, with the vivid blue waters of the inlet under us. To say the view was spectacular is to sell it short.

Then we landed on the beach and had a great lunch prepared by Eleanor. After lunch we proceeded to where the tide was out, buzzed in, and landed a few feet from the receding tidal waters. About ten feet from where we landed, we began picking razor clams, about four or five inches long, with our bare hands. We picked a gunnysack full in about twenty minutes. One of the pilots told us the area yields 1,500 clams per square foot per year. In midafternoon, we flew back to Anchorage and to that mini-airstrip. It was a fabulous trip and a beautiful clear May day. We saw lots of wild game, moose, bear, swans (every lake in the back country of Alaska seemingly has at least one male and female swan).

Before leaving that morning, we had watched John Claus gas up his plane from a stepladder with a five-gallon can and funnel. While this was happening, the other pilot, Gary Pogany, came flying in. His approach was purposely a little high. He put the plane in a slip, a maneuver in flying where the plane drops like a rock but doesn't pick up speed. It looks rather frightening to a non-pilot at close range, and we were right there. At the end of the drop, about five feet off the ground, he flared out and greased in as smooth as glass and screeched to a halt right beside us after a hundred-foot roll. It was a fabulous piece of pilotage but somewhat threatening to an onlooker about to become the next passenger.

Paul took a quick glance at John gassing up the plane with a can and funnel, which was hardly what Paul had expected, then at Gary's plane, which wasn't a DC-10, and at the landing strip, which wasn't O'Hare. He turned to me almost in despair and whispered, "Milt, I hope you know that this trip is your idea." He was really saying, "How in the world could you dream of exposing me to something like this?" When we returned that afternoon, and the polar-air state had magnificently treated us to its very best in weather, visibility, and scenic beauty, all feelings of fear were gone and nothing more was mentioned about who had arranged the trip. In fact, to listen to Paul tell about it later, one would have thought he had arranged the tour himself.

After having been treated to fresh salmon several times, Paul said, on the last day of the trip in Yakutat, "I think we ought to come back here for a full week of fishing; how about it, Milt?" Before I could respond, the mayor of Yakutat said, "Fishing only takes thirty minutes here; what are you going to do the rest of the time?"

Paul must have liked it all very much, because in his contribution to the book of letters given me at my farewell reception as president, he wrote: "I especially enjoyed our many joint trips together and, most of all, from Anchorage in those one-passenger, balloon-tired aircraft to dig razor clams. And in Yakutat where we sat with the mayor, and an Indian chief who gave us the history of one of our missionaries who gave all he had to the Covenant. We ate salmon for four days."

Paul made his own contribution and inspired countless others to follow suit; it was great. I count it a real privilege to have walked, worked, and played with this man.

THE COURAGE TO DREAM

JESSE E. BAILEY

*Jesse E. Bailey is a real-estate broker and owner of
Realty World, LaMesa, California.*

I liked Paul Brandel from the moment of our first meeting. He was warm-hearted and friendly.

Our meeting had been arranged by the Rev. Joseph Broman, retired chaplain of the Swedish National Sanitarium in Denver, a man who seemed to know just about every important Swede in the United States. He had cautioned me that Paul Brandel would probably not be interested in our Spring Valley location for a retirement community. The location and our meager finances might not interest such a person, who had big ideas and a taste for quality.

But as it turned out, Paul was very encouraging. Besides having considerable experience in the area of retirement communities, he had a very positive mental attitude, a term he used many times during our years of working together.

Before our one-hour meeting was over, Paul had authorized me to exercise an option on the seven-acres-plus that we held in Spring Valley, and, to use his words, if we stumbled he would bail us out.

The project we were trying to promote had been started by E. E. Cavallin, a retired railroad worker and a widower who loved San Diego and dreamed of a retirement place for Christians like himself who craved companionship and pleasant surroundings. The name he and his board had selected was the Axie Park Memorial Flower Home Fund.

I had presented the proposal to several organizations, both religious and secular. Most wanted us to turn over the approximately $5,000 we had in cash, with no promise of doing anything. We had finally obtained backing from the California Conference of The Evangelical Covenant Church, but it had considerable reservations and was very willing for Paul Brandel and the Covenant Board of Benevolence to step in.

It is hard to believe that after so short a meeting, Paul Brandel, a Chicago attorney and businessman, could set our sketchy dream on a straight track that would eventually lead to a fully developed retirement community known as Mount Miguel Covenant Village.

I also didn't expect that within a couple of weeks, Paul's secretary, Bernice, would be with me in San Diego, checking out the site and the verbal claims that had been presented. I asked her about Paul's offer to bail us out if we stumbled in our purchase of the property. She quizzed, "Did Paul say that?" Then followed with, "If Paul promised something, you can count on it."

When Paul finally saw the property himself, he perceived it was too small for the project we had in mind. This started the acquisition of approximately twenty adjoining acres, which Paul himself paid for and later donated to the village. I learned that Paul was a man who could make up his mind quickly and not forget what he had committed to.

I soon found myself working with Nils G. Axelson, then administrator of Swedish Covenant Hospital and CEO of the Board of Benevolence. Paul and Nils worked extremely well together, each seeming to know what the other was thinking and doing.

During the years that followed, Paul Brandel became my mentor. I listened to him and tried to follow his every suggestion. My wife, Marian, once irritated by my unmistaken loyalty to Paul, said that if Paul told me to put my hand in a lighted stove, I'd probably do it. I somewhat reluctantly admitted that she was probably right.

At first I used to argue with Paul. At that time I was a community newspaper circulation manager with 1,400 newspaper carriers to supervise. I was strongly opinionated and used to being boss. Paul was a truly humble person. Most of what I knew about his financial holdings had come to me indirectly and were confirmed or modified by Paul when I questioned him. I became aware that he had keen insights on a wide range of subjects and a memory that simply wouldn't quit. He was interested in me and my family, along with his many other associates and friends.

Paul's faith in Christ was strong, and it was matched by his generous giving. He knew Proverbs 11:24,25: "It is possible to give away and become richer! It is also possible to hold on too tightly and lose everything. Yes, the liberal man shall be rich! By watering others, he waters himself" (*The Living Bible*).

There probably was resentment on the part of others when they heard of his contributions, but that didn't deter him. Once he said to me, "I presume you are a tither to your church?" Then he said, "I want to show you what you can do—whatever you give to your church above 10 percent, I'll match."

For the next eighteen months, I doubled my tithe, and Paul matched each amount with periodic checks to my church. We repaired the organ, built new walkways, and completed a number of smaller projects with his matched giving. At last he told me that he had proved that I could give 20 percent, and from then on I was on my own. I couldn't dispute that.

At Paul's and Nils's request, I served for many years on the boards of The Samarkand retirement center in Santa Barbara and of Hearthstone, a proposed retirement community. Those who attended board meetings with Paul were rarely bored. Lively discussions were a hallmark.

Sometimes we drove to San Diego, or to the Los Angeles airport, or from Sacramento to the San Francisco airport. I was often the beneficiary of Paul's philosophies and advice. As we spent time together at all kinds of conferences and business meetings, I became even more aware of Paul's committed giving. I learned that for five consecutive years, he gave away more than his annual income, which set off some interesting Internal Revenue Service inquiries and perhaps some new regulations.

One evening while we were driving to Los Angeles after a Samarkand board meeting in Santa Barbara, Paul started backseat driving. I was at the wheel and the car was full. Paul was laughing, but I wasn't. I would hear him say, "Pass him now," or "Why are you going so slow?" Finally, we reached our favorite coffee shop at Thousand Oaks. When we got out of the car, I handed Paul the keys and said, "It's all yours from now on." He refused the keys, but it ended the backseat driving. Conversation was pleasant during the rest of the ride. That may have been the only time he really got to me.

Paul advocated responsibility in giving. He said don't try to control your contribution after the fact, but use discernment to make your contributions accomplish something. He helped people with their education, in developing their talents, in pursuing their ambitions. I met a number of these persons. Paul spoke many times of using one's time, talents, and treasures. That was his message. That was his practice. That was his legacy.

Before building began for our retirement village, Paul began buying up surrounding property. He would take a map and say, "See what you can do to acquire these lots." I would contact owners, sometimes in distant cities, and try to strike a deal. Much of the land had been subdivided, making for widely scattered ownership, so acquisition was not an easy matter. But Paul had the confidence that we could do it.

Each time I came up with several available properties at reasonable prices, Paul told me to put them into escrow. Sometimes I had to go back and bargain more, explaining to sellers our motives in building a retirement village. If a bigger deposit was required, I'd call Paul, and it would come by mail.

I learned not to write to Paul. If I needed a response, a telephone call to his private line was about the only way to reach him. He almost never answered letters. I knew he read my letters, though, because if he didn't like something, he'd bring it up the next time we met. No answer meant he was too busy or not at home, I never knew which.

I was learning a good deal about real estate and about patience as a bonus. Several times when I became overly concerned about something, I wrote to Bernice. She'd say, "Didn't he answer you?" A few days later I'd get a confirming note from her.

Once when I had a particularly good agreement worked out, Paul said he was short of money and asked if I would put up the needed $5,000. This was in the early 1960s. He knew I earned about $15,000 a year and had only a few hundred dollars in savings. But I answered that I'd try. The next day I went to my bank and, to my surprise, came out with a $5,000 cashier's check. I owned about $6,000 in stocks, and the bank accepted this as collateral. Three months later when the shares dropped a little, the bank asked for more collateral, and I had just enough to cover.

I never asked for the money back, but a few months later at a planning meeting, Paul wrote out a $5,000 check and said thanks. I don't think he realized how relieved I was. I never knew whether he was just testing me or if he really needed the money that much. I never asked.

When the land for the proposed village totaled about twenty-eight acres, and I had a line on more acres from the nearby lake water district, Paul asked me if I didn't think we had enough land. We already had so much more than I ever dreamed of that I answered yes. By then I was experiencing more difficulty from sellers and was surely glad that we had achieved a satisfactory stopping place.

The Covenant Retirement Communities across the country today attest to Paul's foresight and generous giving of his time and means. He had ideas not only on the major policies but on the details that make for better living.

Architects and builders would have surely eliminated walk-in closets and extra storage spaces had it not been for Paul's persistence. He pored over floor plans with a perception not usually associated with board members. As a result, many features not then taken for granted, such as large closets and well-equipped food preparation areas, are present in today's village apartments.

After a board meeting, Paul would often take us out to a good restaurant. If a conversation lagged, he'd start singing the birthday song to me. It didn't matter if it wasn't my birthday. Once I even tried showing my driver's license to a waitress to convince her I didn't rate a birthday candle. Harry Ekstam, one of our favorite administrators, embarrassed me still further by telling the waitress not to pay attention to me because they had just brought me in from "the home." I've had my "birthday" acknowledged at ice-cream parlors and fancy places like the Lauderdale Yacht Club and even the Miami Sheraton, led by opera singer William Harness, with more than 400 persons present. Who could ask for more? I learned to handle embarrassment, and it certainly improved my poise and confidence.

One irritant to me was Paul's many expressions that Florida was better than California. I tried to rebut him by extolling San Diego's great climate. Unbelievably, it rained every time Paul and Nils Axelson came to San Diego. One beautiful cloudless day, I thought I could prove my point. We picked up Paul and Nils at the airport, and before we made it to the place we were meeting, big drops of water were splashing on the windshield. Altogether, it rained or sprinkled the first ten times Paul came to San Diego. Statistics would probably prove that this situation could not be duplicated in a hundred years, since San Diego has only nine and a half inches of annual rainfall.

Obviously, the rain eventually quit, but it gave Paul a strong argument for his Florida-versus-California weather, and provided opening remarks for many of his speeches. When I eventually went to Miami to attend a conference, it was so hot and humid that I decided the trip across town to see a retirement community wasn't worth the effort. I stayed in the hotel where the meetings were held and waited until the next time. Although I knew Paul was teasing, I never got back at him. He had too much ammunition.

When Mount Miguel Covenant Village opened, I was ready to step in as administrator. I went to Illinois and visited Covenant Village of Northbrook, which was newly opened. Paul sat down with me and advised me to consider which would benefit me most: being a manager on the payroll or a person who made his living elsewhere and contributed his time. I decided for the latter.

Before this chapter ends, it is important to show how Paul's influence turned my career. When I first met him, I was a circulation manager for a group of community newspapers. Following my decision to stay with the newspapers, I became production manager and later general manager of a printing company known as Southwest Press and, in fact, publisher of a weekly newspaper group known as the Independent.

Paul advised my wife and me to buy some property with room to subdivide. With some feeling of caution, we did just that. With considerable reservation, we took a small house in trade on our house which we were selling. The small house cost us $18,000, and I was sure we were getting gypped. It seemed the only way to go, however, since the buyer of our former home had to use the smaller house as a down payment. Paul's encouragement in the transaction gave us comfort in our decision to acquire some property.

After five years of management in the newspaper business and the increasing squeezing facing our type of publications, the Chicago owners brought in a publisher and I left. It was a good experience for me, even if difficult. The newspaper and printing operation folded after another five years of intense competition in printing, without the ability to acquire sufficient new high-speed equipment.

Paul advised me to go into real estate. I thought I would do better in the insurance business since I already had the necessary insurance licenses and the promise of some good accounts. Paul's assurance that I had already learned a good deal about real estate and had been through some difficult negotiating to purchase a number of parcels known as assemblage influenced my decision to become a broker.

My earnings for the first year in real estate were more than the combined earnings of my last five years on a salary. Naturally, it wasn't without effort.

My favorite television program was "Gunsmoke," and on Saturday nights I watched Matt Dillon take care of the outlaws and protect the citizens of Dodge City. I polished the family shoes as I watched my favorites, including Doc and Kitty and Chester. But for the next year, "Gunsmoke" lost one of its ardent fans. I was working almost every night, except Sundays. During that time, Paul never failed to encourage me, and his influence kept me working at it.

From the small house we acquired in LaMesa, we traded up to four apartment units, then eight, then sixteen, then twenty-six, and later forty-two. I have to credit the experience to Paul. His frequent references to positive thinking and the money-leverage of other people's money opened my mind to the possibilities available to everyone.

Several years after the death of Paul's wife, Vega, we had the opportunity to congratulate Paul and Bernice while on their honeymoon to San Diego and Lake Tahoe. They stopped at Mount Miguel Covenant Village to visit and assist our first resident, Amy Hederstedt, who needed advice on her dwindling resources.

Many people have commended Paul Brandel for his generosity in giving of his treasure. Probably more important was the tireless use of his talent, and even more the quantity of time, which influenced me and so many others who would listen.

Two additional attributes were his patience and his optimism. He had to practice these qualities to be the philanthropist that he was. If he was overly concerned about what happened to every gift he gave, he surely would have lost some enthusiasm and given less to help others.

Paul Brandel's legacy is indeed a challenge for honesty and for spirited giving. His courage to dream and start big projects dismayed many of his peers, but without his insight, thousands of people would not now be residing in retirement communities across the United States. God was good to us when he sent Paul our way.

PAUL'S NEW MATHEMATICS

LEO WITZ

*Leo Witz, now retired in Scottsdale, Arizona,
was a Chicago entrepreneur and past president and
chairman of the board of Continental Electrical
Construction Company.*

I t was late in September 1949. I was tidying up loose ends at my office since Barbara and I were departing the next day for a long-planned vacation to Italy. I had blocked off my incoming calls, but our switchboard operator cut in on me anyway.

"It's Paul Brandel," she said. "I thought you might want to take it." She knew I would.

I greeted my friend, assuming he was calling to wish us a safe and rewarding trip. Not so. Paul wanted to see me before our departure because he had something he felt would be of extreme interest to me.

"Can you get over here, Leo?" he asked. "I'm at Balmoral (the J. Emil Anderson & Son home base), and I wanted to catch you before you take off. I've got something I think you might want to get into, but it won't wait until you get back. Can you come by before 5:30? I'm stuck here waiting for some calls, and I can't see you later because Vega made a date with some people for dinner."

I hurried through some "must" items, said goodbye to the office personnel, and forty-five minutes after Paul's call was shaking hands with him and waiting for him to enlighten me about the urgency of our meeting.

I left about a half-hour later, the fifty-percent proud owner of a large tract of Florida farmland, the other half vested in J. Emil Anderson & Son.

While in Italy, I came across a gift shop that had some facsimiles of the comedy team of Laurel and Hardy. I acquired a pair and sent

Paul the Hardy doll. I kept the Laurel doll. My accompanying message was, "Dear partner and friend: I trust that we will always be like Damon and Pythias and never like Laurel and Hardy."

For years Hardy was displayed in Paul's office and Laurel in mine.

Through the years, I took equity positions in many of Paul's ventures. Almost all were fruitful. Paul loved to purchase, and he also enjoyed trading property. I used to tease him about his trading proclivities. "Someday," I once told him, "you are going to trade this for that, and that for something else, until you have traded us up to an item worth twenty million dollars—a used submarine."

Paul and I traveled together on business quite often. Whenever we were in Florida, we would visit his mother, who resided at a Covenant retirement center in Miami. She was like a Dresden doll, beautiful and fragile. We would take some of the "girls" out for dinner along with Mother Brandel. None of our dates was younger than ninety. Lest you think this was a mission of conscience, we had joyful, often hilarious, verbal exchanges, and Paul and I thoroughly enjoyed ourselves.

Although the transactions in which I was involved with Paul revolved around vacant real estate, his other acquisitions were in eclectic profusion. They covered banks, Arabian horses, hospitals, nursing homes, farms.

His law office was a mess of organized confusion. In one corner there was a stack of issues of The Wall Street Journal that was literally two feet high. I knew he was never going to find time to read them, and he knew he was never going to get to them, but they stacked up, higher and higher.

Elsewhere in the office there was a conglomeration of unrelated items—African paintings, plaques honoring Paul for various undertakings that benefited humanity, stacks of unanswered communications waiting for the attention that would eventually be directed to them, and folders upon folders of matters pertaining to the contractual necessities of his business ventures. If it were not for the dedicated efforts of Bernice Stege, Paul would not have been able to wander out of the paper swamp he had created.

I always admired Paul for his savoir-faire when faced with situations that would panic mere mortals. He had sublime faith that everything was going to work out all right because of his unshakable con-viction that only providential happenings would follow benevolent conduct.

This dogma, unfortunately, never filtered down to the managers of the mortgage companies, who were frequently the bane of Paul's existence.

Paul Brandel was an acquirer, not generally prone to disposal. This doctrine requires one to disregard normal monetary difficul-ties. Great wealth can be accumulated in fixed assets, such as open land and Arabian horses, but can leave one short of the currency of the realm.

When you have a man of great social conscience, and Paul was the quintessential philanthropist, there were diverse forces tugging at this wonderful person. Paul is the only man I ever knew who would make a pledge of large charitable proportions and then bor-row the money to fulfill his promise.

He always felt he was going in the right direction as long as he continued making ongoing charitable commitments. If he didn't have the funds available at the moment, he soon would, and if nothing materialized to provide him with the necessary capital, he could always get a bank loan until the situation righted itself. On occa-sions when he had a surfeit of funding brought about by the infre-quent selling of one of his assets, Paul would immediately appropriate contributions of the cash bounty to worthy causes.

I have often wondered if Paul's benevolent conduct was totally rational or if it was a positive compulsion with religious overtones. I remember asking him why he made charitable commitments at times when he didn't have the funds available to meet them. My question was selfish in nature, as Paul had sold off one of the parcels in which I had a beneficial interest, and he had not made a distribu-tion of the proceeds.

"I've got a few commitments to clean up, Leo," he said, "and I'll take care of our situation in the near future." Sometimes the near future became the distant future.

The conclusion I have reached concerning Paul's motivations, which governed his philanthropic compulsions, is that he was on a mission to conduct his life in a manner that would richly deserve a high place in heaven. He was content with himself only when he was giving, and his reward while he was still with us was that he was at total peace with himself and his God.

This raises the question whether such fervor should be expected from the rank-and-file of charitably minded individuals. Is it fair to point to a Paul Brandel as a benchmark for giving and expect others to duplicate his intensity of feeling? He was a unique person, and very few are cast in his image. But we can all emulate his intentions. I know that he certainly had a profound effect on me.

I've always been charitably inclined, but Paul's new mathematics opened new horizons for me. He had some monetary equations that would have had the money managers shaking their heads in disbelief.

His theory ran something like this: The first element is that the involved individual must be a person who, out of the goodness of his or her heart, is charitably inclined.

The second element is that said person has achieved a financial comfort zone. This comfort zone has been reached by fortuitous circumstance or many years of earning more than was spent, so that the future holds no fear of dependency upon others for survival.

The third element is the manner in which the capital constituting the comfort zone is invested.

"Let's assume, Leo." Paul informed me, "that you have this surplus of necessary funding which I call your comfort zone, and it is judiciously invested. Let's say that it's in tax-free municipal bonds, AAA, and paying you approximately 7 percent each year. Suppose we use an example of a $100,000 bond, and it generates $7,000 per year in income for you. Your children are adults and well-situated financially, and you're never going to need that $100,000, except to leave it to somebody when you die. Now there's no valid reason for you to hang on to that $100,000 until you die, when you could be giving it to Swedish Covenant Hospital right now, when they really need it. If you give it now, all you are giving away is the use of the $100,000, and that's only $7,000 a year and no big deal."

"Paul," I said, "figures don't lie, but liars figure."

"Then show me what's wrong with what I just told you," he said, and I couldn't. I've been very fortunate and he was right about my financial posture. If I gave $100,000 to a deserving enterprise, I was losing only the use of approximately $7,000 per year, and I was receiving a $30,000 credit on my income-tax return for the year of the gift.

Enough of Paul Brandel rubbed off on me so that my annual "gifting" has increased dramatically through the years. I have no sense of loss at the diminution of my capital reserve, and I experience a sense of well-being and pleasure in the knowledge that I am helping others.

Paul Brandel has gone to his just reward and now lives only in memory. I've shared many experiences with him—comforting him in the grief of losing his wife, Vega, and sharing in the joy of his subsequent marriage.

There is an old adage that says, "When you're gone, you're gone," but that doesn't apply to Paul Brandel. He will always be with us.

Childhood portrait
of Paul Brandel.

Graduation from North
Park Junior College in
1930.

Paul's wedding to Vega
Rundquist in 1938. At left
is Bernice Peterson, now
Bernice Brandel.

Reception at Covenant
Palms of Miami in the
late 1950s shows Paul
Brandel shaking hands
with Anna Anderson,
whose husband, benefactor
Edward Anderson, is in
wheelchair.

Paul's daughter, Carola,
his wife, Vega, and his
mother, Christine, in
1961.

Rainy groundbreaking at Covenant Village of Northbrook in 1964. From left: Joseph C. Danielson, Clarence A. Nelson, Bert Pollak, Paul Brandel, Elmer P. Anderson, and A. Harold Anderson.

Paul presenting diploma to his daughter, Carola, at graduation from Swedish Covenant Hospital's School of Nursing in 1964.

A. Harold and
Lorraine Anderson and
Vega and Paul Brandel
with an award they
received for a prize
bull in the 1960s.

The 1965-66 Covenant Board of Benevolence. From left, seated: Paul Magnuson, Richard
Anderson, Kenneth Gundersen, John Berghoff, C.A. Nelson, Elmer Anderson, Bernice Stege,
Catherine Skanse, Ruth Strandine, Edward Olson.
Standing: Paul Brandel, Carl Olson, Harold Young, John Justema, John Swenson, Lester
Munson, Harold Trittin, Rolland Carlson, Paul Larsen, Stanley Anderson, Walter Johnson, and
Fred Englund.

Paul at reception at time of President Richard Nixon's 1968 inauguration.

Paul and Vega at his fifty-fifth birthday party in 1966, when he received a replica of the Gutenberg Bible.

Paul receiving Salvation Army Bellringer Award in 1970. Chicago's long-time mayor, Richard J. Daley, is second from left.

Paul receiving honorary doctor of laws degree from Illinois Benedictine College in 1974.

Paul, third from right, taking part in dedication of new Immanuel Covenant Church in Stockholm, Sweden, in 1974.

Bernice and Paul at the time of their wedding in 1976.

Margaret and Willard Grant with one of the many station wagons provided for their ministry by Paul Brandel and his friends.

Paul at one of the many picnics he hosted on his farm at Williams Bay, Wisconsin.

Fishing expedition in Upper Michigan includes Ted Roberg III, Dr. Theodore Roberg, Jr., and Paul.

Bernice and Paul with grandchildren, Robert and Kristine, on QE2 cruise in 1978.

Receiving Sweden's Commander of the Royal Order of the North Star award from Consul General Tore Hogstedt in 1979.

Paul and Milton Engebretson pick razor clams in Alaska.

Brandel Manor in Turlock, California, one of several Covenant facilities named in Paul's honor.

Jesse Bailey (left) and Donald Michealsen flank Paul Brandel at groundbreaking for one of the buildings at Mount Miguel Covenant Village.

Wally Lindskoog and Bernice Brandel at Wally's birthday party.

Paul Brandel and W. Clement Stone with Robert C. Byrd, Democratic floor leader of the United States Senate, in 1980.

Nils Axelson and Paul with the president of the Urban League of Miami and the district congressman when Covenant Palms is sold to the Urban League in 1982.

*Paul and Titus Johnson
at the fiftieth
anniversary of
Johnson's missionary
service in Africa.*

*Nils Axelson and Paul
Brandel in 1982.*

Paul is third from right in this
fiftieth-anniversary reunion of his
law-school graduating class in
1983.

Paul and his uncle, David
Brandel, who resides at
Brandel Care Center in
Northbrook, in 1983.

Norma Brandel
Gibbs and Paul in
Lucerne,
Switzerland, in
1983.

Karen Basick has an opportunity to thank Paul Brandel for his kindnesses.

Paul in his Northbrook law office toward the end of his career.

Bernice and Paul when he received the Flame of Leadership Award from the National Council on Youth Leadership in 1984.

Family portrait in 1984. Standing, from left: Kristine, Carola, Loren, and Robert Anderson. Seated: Bernice and Paul.

*Paul and Bernice
Brandel, Milton
Engebretson, and Nils
Axelson at Covenant
Annual Meeting in
1986, when Paul
received special award
for fifty years of
service.*

*The last photo of Paul
was taken a week
before his stroke. He is
shown at Swedish
Covenant Hospital's
centennial celebration
with James B.
McCormick, M.D.,
hospital president.*

Extraordinary Vision for Benevolent Institutions

NILS G. AXELSON

*Nils G. Axelson is president of Covenant Benevolent
Institutions, a department of The Evangelical Covenant
Church that includes two hospitals and twelve
Covenant retirement communities.*

The remarkable Paul W. Brandel was a man of extraordinary
vision who saw himself as God's steward of whatever possessions came his way. In his particular affinity for The Evangelical Covenant Church, every area of the church's ministry was
blessed by his generosity. Not least was the way he used his time,
talent, and treasure on behalf of Covenant Benevolent Institutions.

His involvement with the Board of Benevolence began in 1938
when, as a relatively new member of the legal bar association, he
was the youngest member to be elected to the board.

My first association with him occurred during the summer of 1952,
shortly after my arrival as the new administrator of Covenant Benevolent Institutions. As the CEO of Swedish Covenant Hospital and
Covenant Home, my time and attention were absorbed by many
important matters requiring immediate attention. Among them were
incessant requests from the Illinois Department of Public Health
and a major Chicago bank for current status reports, then behind
schedule, on our building of Nelson Hall. Financing was a combination of a government grant and a bank construction loan.

Immersed as I was with these problems, it was disconcerting to
find that adjunct to our institutional program was a fledgling retirement community in Florida called Covenant Palms of Miami. With
twenty-five people in residence, a crisis was developing, and our principal benefactor was becoming impatient and threatening to walk
out on us.

A quick consultation with the Board of Benevolence resulted in a decision to designate a liaison person for Covenant Palms. After considering three individuals who were familiar with the Florida project and personally acquainted with our benefactor, Edward Anderson, there was a unanimous decision to appoint Paul Brandel. Paul agreed to commit the time required. For him, acceptance of this appointment was but a part of his sense of a larger design for service.

As Paul and I ventured forth on behalf of Covenant Palms, little did I realize the importance of this turn of events in my life and to Covenant Benevolent Institutions. To my everlasting gratitude, I found in Paul a colleague, a collaborator, an ally, a conferee, a mentor, and, above all, a friend.

Initially I wondered how I would get along with this person who often expressed conservative, traditional, authoritative, exasperating views. But before long I was excited by his creativity and his ingenious approach to problems. His often unorthodox approach usually found my enthusiastic response. It was possible to disagree and even become irritated or annoyed, yet this did not result in animosity. There was always enough respect for the other person's views to reach accord. Indeed, under a conservative and seemingly authoritative stance lurked a man whose soul had found a purpose in life. His spiritual strength had its own presence as he sought to give of himself ever more generously.

For a time, we visited Covenant Palms on a monthly basis. Our meetings around Edward Anderson's dining room table seemed to occupy endless hours. In Edward's view, no detail was insignificant. In many ways he and Paul were kindred spirits. In the management of whatever wealth they had acquired, Edward and his wife, Anna, also saw their role as stewards of what properly belonged to God.

The rapport established between Edward Anderson and Paul Brandel resulted in the Andersons providing additional contributions to Covenant Palms. Sometimes Edward would offer, with almost impish delight, to provide funds for two more cottages if Paul would come up with the money for a third.

Paul always responded positively to this kind of challenge—even when he had no idea where the cash would come from. It was not unlike Paul to overextend himself with pledges to Covenant causes. Inevitably, however, something would come up to provide the cash to meet his commitment. An overdue loan that Paul had written off was suddenly paid in full; an insurance policy matured and the cash was available; a building lot that had languished for years was suddenly in a hot real-estate market. To Paul, these occurrences were not unusual, because he gave not only on the basis of what he had but with the faith and hope that there would always be even more to give.

As we closed the chapter on Covenant Palms with its sale to the Urban League of Miami, it was Paul again who did so much to facilitate the sale, even though, as the second largest benefactor to Covenant Palms, he had held dreams of the possibility of continuing to operate it.

Although the continuation of Covenant Palms in Miami may at times have been a matter of differing opinions, the concept of a second location in Florida for a Covenant retirement community was broached more than twenty years ago. A former chief executive officer of Covenant Palms was charged with the responsibility of identifying a possible second location. As time passed without definitive action, it was Paul Brandel who again worked with us in evaluating possibilities in Pompano Beach and Boynton Beach. Finally, our considerable efforts centered on a Baptist project in Plantation, Florida, that was in financial distress.

After negotiating with bank officials in Indianapolis, they agreed to Paul's request to discount the mortgage by $1 million. First National Bank of Chicago assisted us by buying out the mortgage. This venture provided the basic site for the relocation of Covenant Palms and the expansion of our Florida work at Plantation.

Our experience at Covenant Palms and the withdrawal of approval for a Covenant-wide campaign to benefit Covenant Home and the various conference homes for the aged prompted review of other possible options.

This review resulted in our developing the concept for Covenant Village of Northbrook. Although the first attempt to receive board approval was unsuccessful, this only motivated us to prepare a better feasibility study. Since Paul's visionary statements sometimes confused people, I suggested this was a little like speaking in tongues and offered to be the interpreter. Again, by collaborating we were able to provide the board with an unassailable presentation, not least of which was the question of site.

Paul had identified five sites that were available or on option. He had personally extended his own resources to present these locations. After the board gave approval to the concept and the Northbrook site, Paul donated his interest in it. He also obtained donations from A. Harold Anderson, Dr. Edward Millar, and Dr. William F. Hutson. Ultimately, this site was expanded to about sixty acres, with three acres donated to the Northbrook YMCA, three acres to the Northbrook Evangelical Covenant Church, and two acres for parking for the church and the Y.

As discussions were proceeding on the Northbrook project, Dr. K. M. Nelson of Princeton, Illinois, a Board of Benevolence member, invited the board to hold a retreat at Starved Rock State Park. During that meeting, we received a phone call from the Rev. Gordon Nelson, then superintendent of the California Conference (now Pacific Southwest Conference). He inquired whether the board would consider becoming involved with a Covenant Palms West. He said that Jesse Bailey, a member of First Covenant Church of San Diego, was chair of a committee that was ready to make a down payment on some land near the Mount Miguel Covenant Church. We agreed to explore this project.

After an initial visit to the proposed site in Spring Valley, Paul advised Jesse Bailey that the site was inadequate. But since there was adjoining vacant land, he instructed Jesse to acquire more land, saying, "Let me know what you need and I will provide it."

This story and that of the development of Mount Miguel Covenant Village is told in another chapter of this book. Of course, in commending Paul's spirit of stewardship, we must also recognize Jesse's considerable contributions. He came to value, as did so many others, that Paul's word was his bond. Paul exemplified a statement for which John D. Rockefeller is given credit: "I believe in the sacredness of a promise, that a man's word should be as good as his bond; that character—not wealth or power or position—is of supreme worth."

Early in his ministry, during his pastorate at the Orangevale Covenant Church, the Rev. Paul E. Larsen introduced us to the indefatigable Fayetta Philip—the oldest woman pharmacist in California at that time, a lapidarian, a Shakespearean collector, a realtor, a lobbyist, and a self-styled authority on planning retirement housing. Fayetta's dream of developing retirement housing at Folsom, California, had begun with the acquisition of land and the construction of a building with a few model apartments.

As Paul Larsen, Robert H. Peterson, Bernice Brandel, and others can attest, Paul Brandel gave unstintingly of his time to bring about the development of Hearthstone Manor, but other forces were on the horizon. The board of Bethany Home in Turlock was seeking to replace its outmoded facilities. A few years earlier, Paul and I had visited the old Emanuel Hospital in Turlock and had met with its board of directors. During that visit, we were provided overnight housing at Bethany Home. Afterwards, Paul often chortled as he spoke of sleeping on an iron bed at Bethany.

Fortunately, the hospital board responded to our suggestions, and a new building replaced the original hospital. Subsequently, we agreed to accept the transfer of the hospital and the two homes—Bethany in Turlock and Elim in Tujunga. With these new considerations, we decided to discontinue the Hearthstone Manor project in Folsom.

After reviewing the Bethany Home facility, we decided to move ahead with a retirement center to be called Covenant Village of Turlock. Paul enlisted Donald Michealsen's assistance, and they donated the new site. Later, Don and Paul arranged for a favorable disposition of the Folsom property and also donated to the Covenant the Brandel Manor nursing-care facility in Turlock.

The Samarkand in Santa Barbara, California, was a financially troubled retirement center. Sidney Rasanen, a staff member at Westmont College in Santa Barbara and later a financial officer at North Park College, knew of Samarkand's problems. He suggested that the Samarkand board invite Paul Brandel and me to visit the place and offer suggestions. Our visit resulted in an invitation to join the board of directors, a request that was submitted to the Board of Benevolence for approval. Within two years, a further request was made to the Board of Benevolence and to the Covenant Executive Board to accept Samarkand as a Covenant Benevolent Institution.

Although Samarkand was financially distressed, the potential for a successful operation was obvious. To avoid risk to the Covenant, Paul stepped in to personally guarantee Samarkand obligations. One year after its acceptance as a Covenant retirement facility, and with

Harry Ekstam as the chief executive officer, we were on the way to a turnaround. By underwriting the financial obligations, Paul not only evidenced his stewardship commitment but demonstrated his faith in the management resources available to get the job done.

In Cromwell, Connecticut, we have a variation on the theme in the development of Pilgrim Manor. This was an East Coast Conference project that replaced the home for the aged located in the Bronx, New York. I had a brief stint with this home as vacation relief for the administrator in the summer of 1949.

Over the years, Paul and I had met with the board, first in the Bronx and later at Cromwell. At one of these meetings, a board member inquired, "Since you're willing to meet with us and share your knowledge and experience, what difference would it make if we were under the aegis of the Board of Benevolence?" Paul's rejoinder was, "If you were under the aegis of the Board of Benevolence, it would be more difficult to ignore our suggestions." Unreasonable terms required by an insurance company in order to provide mortgage financing subsequently brought the Cromwell facility, which later developed into Covenant Village of Cromwell and Pilgrim Manor, under the arm of the Board of Benevolence.

The Holmstad retirement community in Batavia, Illinois, began with the formation of a State of Illinois not-for-profit corporation with a board of directors composed of Covenant church members. This project was also endorsed by the Evangelical Covenant Church in Batavia. The land for this center, valued at $1,000,000, was donated by Paul Brandel. With the feasibility assured, with the first twenty-five or thirty residents in place, and with Harry Ekstam again in charge, Paul was comfortable in recommending transfer to the Board of Benevolence.

Over the years, there were numerous other prospective ventures and contributions of time and travel expense. They included visits on behalf of the Frewsburg Home in New York and visits to Jamestown, Chautauqua, and Youngstown. There was a proposed Iowa Home at Dayton. Since there was no doctor, much less any health care facility in Dayton, this was not viewed as an appropriate location. The Valley View project in which the First Covenant Church of Des Moines was involved was a better concept. There were also numerous visits and discussions regarding a North Pacific retirement center at Tacoma and in other locations.

In these and other instances, Paul was willing to respond to requests from appropriate Covenant sources but was disappointed if there were no signs of local commitment. Initial discussions in Colorado resulted in acquisition of property, but failure to acquire adjacent land resulted in its purchase by a cemetery organization. It became somewhat incongruous to consider a cemetery as an immediate neighbor! A loan for this project from a conference development fund was called for other purposes. And a request for the names of specific individuals who would agree to apply resulted in no names.

Although this project did not proceed, Paul demonstrated his willingness to give of his time, to absorb travel and other expenses, and to exhort others to give of their time and means to a potential Covenant endeavor. The concept of a Colorado retirement community continues to survive, and a committee endorsed by the Midwest Conference is currently active.

In discussing Paul's relationship to Covenant Benevolent Institutions, we must also call attention to his five decades of service to Swedish Covenant Hospital. During this time, all major fundraising activities were successful because of his direct participation. Of course there were many other volunteers and campaign workers as well as important gifts from many sources, including the Service Guild, the Witz family, A. Harold Anderson, W. Clement Stone, and a host of others. It was Paul's personal commitment, however, his gentle prodding of others, his continuing optimism, and his unfaltering leadership that brought the desired results.

Although Paul was inextricably involved with our retirement centers and their development, and we could not have proceeded without him, he also gave of himself to a variety of other Covenant efforts.

Senior Adult Ministries Implemented, although initiated by the Covenant Social Services Institutions Commission, was influenced and assisted by Paul. A commission survey brought an unparalleled response from Covenant pastors asking for programming to assist congregations in their ministry to senior adults. The commission's efforts centered on enlisting younger retirees in a congregation to invest their time and services to provide assistance to older seniors.

The commission sought the advice of Milton Engebretson and Paul Brandel. Since it was limited to a budget of only $1,000 per year, there was also the hope of more funding.

As he listened to a presentation by LeRoy A. Benson, Harry Ekstam, and Paul W. Peterson at a meeting which he hosted, Paul was most responsive. He was immediately attracted by the opportunities this concept presented. Before discussing additional funding, however, Paul challenged the committee to assemble a volunteer staff and to prepare a prototype seminar that could be presented in a number of Covenant churches.

The commission proceeded to organize a panel of persons who developed a format for a weekend seminar. The seminar was presented at Covenant churches in New Britain, Connecticut; Chicago; Minneapolis; Pomeroy, Iowa; and Redwood City, California. Paul assisted the commission in its efforts to review and report the results.

The Covenant Department of Christian Education and Discipleship embraced the commission's efforts and invited participation at Scene '78 at Big Sky, Montana. A regular meeting of the Board of Benevolence was scheduled at Big Sky, and board members were urged to remain for the SAMI sessions.

As the SAMI concept developed, Paul arranged to allocate a portion of a $1 million gift which he had presented to The Evangelical Covenant Church. With some funding assured, Paul W. Peterson, who had retired as administrator of Covenant Palms, undertook major responsibility for SAMI, including publishing resource material to be used as study guides in Covenant churches.

Today, the SAMI program continues in various ways. The Department of Christian Education and Discipleship is holding the third Fifty Plus Conference in July 1990. Sylvia Peterson continues to edit a newsletter distributed by the department. Harry Ekstam has held meetings with groups of seniors and church staffs in Pasadena, Grand Rapids, and elsewhere. Continuation of the SAMI program is assured in a provision by Bernice Brandel for an endowment to maintain funding for this purpose.

Paul's efforts on behalf of North Park College and Theological Seminary have taken many forms over the years. He served as chairman of the Finish and Furnish campaign at the time of the construction of Carlson Tower. He was an active alumnus, consultant to the Board of Directors, and a generous benefactor on many occasions, including endowing a chair in nursing education. In the fall of 1989, another endowed chair, the Paul W. Brandel Chair in New Testament Studies, was instituted at the seminary. He received a distinguished alumnus award and an honorary doctor of laws degree from North Park.

His continuing interest and involvement in missions is exemplified by his providing funds to assist in the acquisition of a special breed of cattle for the Paul Carlson hospital campus in Zaire which I, if no one else, termed the "Titus Johnson/Paul Brandel Cattle Ranch." This was an effort to assist the hospital to become self-sufficient in its meat supply in an area where the diet was protein deficient.

A discourse on Paul Brandel would be incomplete without calling attention to his unfailing sense of humor. He liked to tease, and he also responded well to being teased. Ask Edward L. Olson about the elks' bugling in Colorado. Ask Jesse Bailey how many birthdays you can have in one year. Ask Ralph Hanson, Fernly Johnson, or me about our discovery that golf can include not only mulligans but Brandeligans. Ask Dr. William Hutson, who knew about hunting, fishing, and photographic expeditions, how he was introduced to eating expeditions. When it came to fishing, which was serious business with Paul and almost inviolable, there were also occasions for frivolity. Just ask me or someone else whose views, like mine, are not sacrosanct.

Paul had many favorite sayings that he quoted often. Among them were, "Blessed are the short-winded, for they shall be called upon again." And "Blessed are those who go around in circles, for they shall be called big wheels."

I recall Paul's delight in giving an unexpected answer to an inquiry from an unsuspecting person. When a clerk at the car-rental desk at the San Francisco airport asked for Paul's destination, he said, with a twinkle in his eye, "Well, first we go to Divine Gardens and then to Tickle Pink." The response was, "Please, where are you going to be staying?" The clerk, of course, did not know about the motel Divine Gardens in Turlock, then owned by Mr. Divinian, or the motel at Carmel owned by Mr. Tickle.

In his book, *Thanks Be to God*, Robert N. Rodenmayer distinguishes between "grudge giving," "duty giving," and "thanks giving." "The first comes from constraint, the second from a sense of obligation, the third from a full heart." For Paul Brandel, his course of action was all thanks giving: "a life lived in thanksgiving because God has been and continues to be so good to us." It was Paul's constant view that "no matter what we give, we cannot outgive the Lord."

Covenant Benevolent Institutions have been extraordinarily blessed by Paul Brandel's vision and generous giving.

SAGE WISDOM AND WISE COUNSEL

RODNEY K. JOHNSON

Rodney K. Johnson is an attorney-at-law in the firm Brandel and Johnson, Northbrook, Illinois.

I spent nearly twenty-five years of my life working with Paul Brandel, and it would be most unusual if the influence of a man of his depth of character, his abilities, and his generosity did not have a profound impact on my life.

I had known Paul since my childhood in the Edgebrook Covenant Church in Chicago, but I had never really considered working with him. During the spring of 1961, prior to graduation from Northwestern University School of Law, I had been interviewing with law firms, banks, and the other places law-school graduates look for jobs, but had not settled on any particular one.

In June, just after graduation, my fiancee, Corene, and I were invited by Paul, along with a number of other guests, for a Lake Michigan dinner cruise on the yacht *Janice*, which Paul and A. Harold Anderson owned.

Paul was aware that I was studying for the bar exam, and he simply said, "How would you like to work in my office?" I said "Yes," and Paul said, "Come in October 1." That was it. It was probably the shortest job interview anyone ever had.

When I began working with Paul, I had just passed the bar exam and been admitted to the practice of law in the State of Illinois. I soon became aware that very little I had been taught in my legal education had prepared me for the real world of law practice with Paul.

The academic world was precise, controlled, even peaceful. Paul's office was just the opposite, with a multitude of things happening all at once—phones constantly ringing, people running to meet deadlines, constant deadlines, and Paul in the middle of all this confusion, making decisions, making things happen, and constantly on the phone. My first impressions centered on wondering how I would ever adapt to this type of life and working environment.

Paul's basic assumption was that those who worked with him had to be strong and self-reliant and willing to learn things for themselves. This meant go do it, learn quickly, do it right, sink or swim. This was Paul's way of educating a person, also his way of finding out if you were the type of person he could effectively work with. He didn't have the time to stand over someone while the person learned, and I think he deeply believed this format was also essential for the person learning. Somehow, over the years, as I reflect on all that has occurred, I believe he was right.

Paul liked to dress right. Right meant a suit, white shirt, tie, and brightly shined shoes. Shirts had to be long-sleeved, even in summer. Paul followed his dress code to a T—always. There is a photo in existence, I will not say where, of Paul walking on Waikiki Beach in a white shirt, dark trousers, and shiny black shoes. The tie is missing in deference to the tropics.

Being young and inexperienced, I didn't take Paul's instructions too seriously. About two weeks after I began working, I made the error of coming to work in a sport coat and slacks. Needless to say, I did not make this mistake again. Paul let me know, in terms not too dissimilar to that of a law-school professor, what was expected of me in his office.

During the early 1960s, Paul's interest in education led him to teach a business law class at North Park College. Almost at once this became one of the most popular evening-school courses. This was also my introduction to teaching since Paul's schedule did not always allow him to make the class. Paul did not teach theory. Rather he told stories and drew from experiences in his life and legal practice to make his points. The students loved these sessions, and absences were few.

In order to make the class more interesting, and also to accommodate his schedule, Paul often brought in as guest lecturers some of his more interesting friends in the real-estate business. One who particularly comes to mind was Andy Sakelson, a real-estate broker and promoter who had over the years brought many deals to Paul. Sakelson was a man of great vision and one who made no small plans. Things didn't always happen the way he envisioned, but the prospects were always great and he could tell the best stories. Sakelson knew the great architect Frank Lloyd Wright and talked about working with him on the "mile high" building project Wright was promoting on the Illinois Central air rights during the 1950s. When Paul and Sakelson got going with the class on this subject, it made for an unforgettable evening.

Paul brought in other guest lecturers, each one more impressive than the other. They didn't teach much law, but the students received a great education in how some of the great real-estate promoters of the day did business. Paul let me and several others teach "the law." The fact was that Paul didn't really intend to teach a comprehensive course in law. Rather, it was his goal to interest and motivate the students to pursue law as a profession. Interestingly, a number of students in these classes did go on to become attorneys, and several have told me that their interest in the profession originated with Paul's teaching.

Paul had an uncanny sense of vision when it came to buying land. I can recall his interest in the early 1960s in the intersection of Route 53 and I-90, the land which was ultimately to become the location of the Woodfield Mall shopping center. Very quietly and with no fanfare, Paul began purchasing acreage at the southwest corner of this intersection from the various owners, who were, in most cases, still farming the land.

I can remember sitting with Paul in the kitchens of several farmhouses with the farmers and their families, drinking coffee—always coffee—while he patiently reached agreement with these folks. It wasn't long until he controlled all the key tracts of land.

Paul had an associate in his office named Archie Siegal. Archie was a lawyer and real-estate broker who had connections with the real-estate division of Sears. He was also a very intense guy. He loved to tell Paul about all the big deals he was involved in, and now he had the biggest one of his life. He explained how Sears was searching for just the right spot to locate the largest enclosed shopping mall ever built and that he was leading the search for the site.

A short time later, Archie told Paul that the site had been located.

Sure enough, it was the same land Paul had been acquiring. Paul saw this as an opportunity for some great entertainment and said nothing to Archie about his acquisition of the property. It wasn't long before Archie, his blood-pressure at its upper limits, charged into Paul's office. On his first visit to one of the farmers he had been told, "You're too late; I just sold to a guy named Paul Brandel." Paul, with his famous cherubic grin, told Archie, "Why didn't you come and see me first? I could have saved you the pain and frustration."

Needless to say, a deal was made, and Paul and A. Harold Anderson became a part of the creation of Woodfield Mall—the largest shopping mall ever built up to that time—and of the development of many hundreds of acres surrounding it.

Paul always kept an appointment book, his "black book" he called it. It contained his schedule for everything he had to do, and he always had it in his pocket. It was this book that enabled him to keep some semblance of sense and order in an otherwise hectic existence.

Business appointments, breakfasts, lunches, dinners, business trips, vacations, deadlines—everything Paul did and was going to do— was logged in this book. He relied on it absolutely, and I never heard of him losing one in all the years I worked with him. I shudder to think what might have happened or what might not have happened if the black book had been lost.

Paul always had time for his friends and was ready to meet with them and assist in the solution of their legal and personal problems. These problems might have been small compared to the matters Paul was dealing with every day, but he was a man of great heart and compassion and realized that when a friend or client had a problem it was a serious matter to that person.

House closings, wills, estates, adoptions, business and financial advice, and all the other areas of general legal practice were handled by Paul for a multitude of friends and clients over the years. Paul, in his usual generosity, often charged less than the regular fee and in some cases nothing, depending on the client's ability to pay. Paul did all of this for many years, along with the large real-estate development and construction projects that were the primary focus of his law practice and business.

Another less known but equally important aspect of Paul's great generosity was the financial help he bestowed on countless individuals whose needs came to his attention. College educations, cars, jobs, and every kind of help you could imagine were dispensed by Paul on a continuing and ongoing basis. His Christmas lists included the names of many pastors and missionaries who received monetary gifts each year. This was always done in private and was unknown to most people in Paul's world.

His attitude was that since he had been blessed financially, it was his duty and obligation to help others. He never helped with the expectation of being repaid. Sometimes he was, often he was not, but this never affected his generosity.

Paul's generosity and sense of stewardship toward Covenant causes and those of other Christian and secular groups are well known. In the representation of his clients, Paul always encouraged them verbally and, in particular, by his own example to be generous and benevolent regarding the charitable things of this life and especially Christian causes and the needs of The Evangelical Covenant Church. When it came to generosity, Paul practiced what most people only talk about, and in the process he became an example of a truly great steward.

He was much more than an attorney. He was foremost a counselor, and friends came to him as often for his advice with the problems of life as they did for specific legal problems. He was always ready to give advice and counsel. Sometimes the friends and associates who were the recipients of his advice were not particularly pleased to be on the receiving end of his sage wisdom.

I must admit, however, that in working with Paul for nearly twenty-five years, I found the advice he gave to clients and to me, in the vast majority of cases, to be wise and accurate, and those who had the wisdom to follow his advice were usually well-rewarded by the outcome.

These are but a few of my memories of my years with Paul. He was a truly rare human being. He was blessed with a vision of what is good, what is right, and what should be done, and he had the will and determination to make it happen. I consider myself honored and blessed to have known him all my life and to have worked with him for so many years.

KEEPING THE WHEELS ROLLING

MARGARET GRANT

Margaret Grant and her husband, Willard, direct Creative Evangelism, Inc., a national children's ministry headquartered in Clifton, Kansas.

Y ou stay in Chicago, Margaret, and let Willard take the train to New England alone," said Paul Brandel in his blunt way. "He can get the station wagon and trailer and bring it back without your help." Saddened by my father's serious illness and weary from our twenty-four-hour journey trying to reach my parents' home in Illinois from Boston, Massachusetts, I burst into tears.

Paul, with a look of tender concern on his face, quickly apologized and said, "Go with Willard; it's all right."

Such direction was coming from a friend who had known my family since his birth. And before that, his mother, as a young immigrant from Sweden, had lived in my grandparents' home in the Englewood area of Chicago. Paul's parents and my father had been friends since before any of them had married. Paul was carried in his mother's arms to a Swedish Methodist church on South Racine Avenue in an area of Chicago heavily populated by Swedes. His first Sunday-school superintendent was my father, Charles R. Palmquist.

Many decades later, in 1954, Paul was the Sunday-school superintendent at the Edgebrook Covenant Church in northwest Chicago. Willard and I were being interviewed for the job of youth directors, and Paul was outlining the required tasks.

I responded, "I understand. It's what I'm used to in Sunday school. My dad always did things that way."

"What's your maiden name?" Paul asked.

"Palmquist," I replied.

"Charlie's daughter?"

I nodded yes.

"Do it exactly like your father did and I'll never tell you another thing." And he didn't.

The way we did our work brought great joy to Paul. He began to prod us to go nationwide in a full-time evangelistic youth ministry.

Three months prior to Willard's graduation from North Park Theological Seminary in 1955, the Lord closed the doors to Taiwan for us. Ten years of schooling preparing to be missionaries seemed all for naught. Out of this turn of events, however, many people, of whom Paul was chief, urged us to embark on a children's ministry.

After Willard announced at his interview with the Covenant conference superintendents that by faith we would enter such a ministry, Paul was the first person to contact us. "Give me a list of everything you will need, and I will try to raise some money for you."

We made the list quickly. In a few days Paul called and said, "Go to Sessler Ford and order a red-and-white station wagon."

"But Paul," Willard stammered, "we don't even have enough bus fare to get out to Sessler. How can we order a station wagon?"

"Do as I tell you," was Paul's quick retort. "Trust me and trust God." This was one of the first times through the more than three decades that followed that we would hear quick unhesitating instructions from Paul. He was second only to my father in giving earthly advice. We would someday find no way to fill the void when this great friend would be called home.

A week before graduation, Paul returned from an extended business trip and handed us a check for $500. "I've been unable to raise money because I've been away. But take this and get what you can."

This amount bought many items in 1955. Tires were put on a utility trailer we had purchased, and insurance was provided for our vehicles and the extensive equipment our theme approach entailed. No amount of pleading with Paul for the names of the donors was successful. "We can't do your work, but we can see that you have the tools to do it," he always said.

Tears of joy rolled down our cheeks, and Willard said, "I hope we never do anything to disappoint you." Tenderly came the reply, "That's all I can ask."

Somehow, some way, Paul and his friends supplied thirteen vehicles for our use through the years. We don't know all whom he enlisted. The vehicles were returned when we could no longer keep them in repair, and another one would miraculously appear. The thirteenth car was given to Creative Evangelism, Inc., with the instruction from its three donors—Paul Brandel, A. Harold Anderson, and Wally Lindskoog—that in faith we put away $5,000 each year toward its replacement. God's timing was perfect. The one who made sure wheels were rolling under us had gone to be with the Lord by the time the fourteenth car was purchased.

Paul had promised in June 1955 that he would stand behind us, that if ever a need arose, we were to tell him and he would help us. We made a point of never asking him for a cent. Just getting insured vehicles to use made us very grateful.

In 1962 when we thought my father was dying, my mother summoned us home to Hinsdale, Illinois. Our meetings in Waltham, Massachusetts, had to be cancelled. Our station wagon and trailer needed to be retrieved so our schedule could continue. It was at this time that Paul wanted Willard to make the trip alone.

When my dad did die four months later, our friend, Paul Brandel, took his place. Like a family member, he paid for our daughter Maureen's confirmation dress. As confirmation day came to a close, the Brandels whispered, "She's like an angel."

Paul and Vega were Maureen's legal guardians. Life on the road bore the risk of accident, and we wanted to be sure there would be someone to look after her.

Once when we told Paul that Maureen would join us in California for Christmas, he asked, "She's flying, isn't she?"

"No," I responded, "the train is cheaper."

"And more dangerous," was his steel-like reply. "Three days alone on a train for a ten-year-old is ridiculous. Here, I'll pay for the plane ticket this time, and after this make sure you save enough money for her to fly."

"Thank you, Paul. We will remember your advice," promised Willard, and we did.

Maureen was cognizant even at that age of the unusual things Paul did for God's servants—always with the insistence that he not be thanked publicly for his kindness. "I don't want any thanks from you. I want it from the Lord, and I can wait until I get to heaven."

She remembered the doctor in Montana who discovered I was suffering from high blood pressure at the age of thirty-three. He instituted a rigid diet that brought me down four dress sizes in six months. We had been saving to buy new clothes for me and a new topcoat for Willard upon our return to Chicago. But the station wagon we were driving broke down every day on the journey from California. Repair bills took all we had saved and more.

We went to church the next Sunday in my too-big coat and Willard in his worn-out topcoat. The next morning, my mother, a trained seamstress, was pinning my coat in an attempt to make it smaller. She was also trimming off the worn cuffs on Willard's coat. Laughing, we said he would be the only preacher in the Covenant with a coat with three-fourths-length sleeves.

The ringing of the phone interrupted our task. The Brandels had seen us in church and were so pleased with my weight loss. Could I meet Mrs. Brandel at Marshall Field's the next day? They wanted to buy me a new coat.

While we ladies shopped, Willard was to wait at Paul's office. We would meet for lunch in the Walnut Room. A fur coat was offered to me, which I promptly refused; our ministry took us to many poor areas. So I chose a simple black cloth coat as well as a hat and gloves. Then came the offer of a dress or suit.

After pondering awhile, I said, "I've never had anything but second-hand suits from my aunt; a new suit would be marvelous." I was gently steered to a special room where the clerk looked at me for a moment and then returned with a high-fashion suit the buyer had just secured from Ireland. I loved it, and the suit became mine.

When we met Willard, he too was carrying a box. Paul had sent a lawyer-friend with Willard to Hart Schaffner & Marx to buy a new topcoat. The lawyer suggested a cashmere coat which Willard refused—too fancy for an evangelist. But the lawyer made the decision. Many of you have hung that cashmere-blend coat in your closet when we have visited your home.

On that errand the lawyer told Willard, "Brandel has changed my vocabulary. When I first met him, every other word I used was a swear word. He told me I wasn't very intelligent; I didn't know enough words to speak correctly." Brandel the benefactor was also Brandel the constant witness.

Maureen also remembered the day we were leaving for the West Coast, and our funds were very low. Willard went to Swedish Covenant Hospital to visit a friend and found Paul there. Paul, in his usual exuberant way, announced, "Ten percent of the contents of each one's wallet for Willard and Margaret." Again, our need was met by Paul's natural gesture of sharing while training others to do the same.

In the midst of seeing Uncle Paul unselfishly at work in the lives of many people, Maureen heard that some people questioned his motives. It prompted her to write an essay about this great man and all he did for God, mostly without letting people know he was the giver. She got an A on her paper. I found it in her school books a few months later when we returned from our crusades.

Unknown to her, I mailed it to Paul's office. We later heard from his wife that this essay became one of his treasures. Whenever he was utterly discouraged, he would read the words penned by a child's hand, constructed by a child's heart. Renewed and encouraged, he would go on to give even more to the Lord's work.

We and our parents were concerned about Maureen's schooling. We investigated Christian high schools with boarding facilities and found the cost prohibitive. A Nebraska farm family who had been classmates of ours at North Park offered to keep Maureen. But Uncle Paul was also concerned and offered a complete scholarship for her at Wheaton Academy, West Chicago, Illinois. This was followed by a supplementary scholarship for her at North Park College. What Paul and some of his friends did not provide, the State of Illinois did.

Maureen had a key to the Brandel house and an invitation to go there whenever she wished. Her high-school graduation reception was held in that elegant home. When she was planning her wedding, we were in a quandary where to hold it. Our home church, Edgebrook Covenant, was too small. Then the Brandels stepped in. They suggested that we have the wedding at a large Methodist church and the reception at the Michigan Shores Club. Aghast, we said, "We can't afford those places."

"Who said anything about money?" Paul declared. "Make the arrangements, and I'll take care of the bills." He told us to tip the janitor of the church and buy Maureen's shoes. And so the young lady who never had her own home had the wedding of a princess because she had an Uncle Paul.

That same year Paul was contacted by the Church Union of Hong Kong—about 140 churches of all denominations. They asked him to pay our way to Hong Kong to hold children's crusades. He agreed to do this and then informed us of the commitment. He also wanted us to spend one month in Japan and one month in Taiwan holding crusades in Covenant churches. He suggested we spend two months prior to the meetings in Hong Kong making our equipment, thereby enabling us to leave our regular things in America.

Paul was elated with the plans, for it had been his secret desire to send Willard back home to Hong Kong for an extended visit. We could accomplish service to Christ along with a visit with Willard's adopted Chinese brothers and sisters. Paul paid all flight expenses and for the needed electronic equipment. We were without an income for five months but were thrilled with the opportunity to reach children of the Orient for Christ.

Three years earlier, upon hearing that Willard had been diagnosed hypoglycemic, Paul had sent us to Europe accompanying the North Park College Choir. More tour members were needed for the chartered flights, and Willard needed a rest. God through Paul met both needs.

Often when spending time with the Brandels we would discuss our motivation for giving to the Lord. Paul would always say that he tithed this year what he wanted to make next year. Sometimes this would bring a frown to my face, and Paul would remind me that the Bible says nothing about motives. Just give and it will be returned to you. He must have felt he was having difficulty convincing me because he queried, "You want to be rich, don't you, Margaret?"

I literally recoiled. Of course I didn't want to be rich. It was unholy. How many sermons had I heard about the evil rich man? Paul must have read my thoughts, for he bounced back with, "Shame on you. It is the duty of every Christian to try to be rich—so he can give back to God."

I should have known Paul's motives would be right. Was I not talking to the richest person I knew? And he was not evil. I once heard someone assail him at a Christian institution, "Why don't you give us a piano?" Paul didn't answer, "I have given over $50,000 worth of furniture for this room." Instead he smiled and said, "Maybe someday you will get a piano."

This was the man who told us not to stop our work to care for our parents. It was more important that we win children for Christ. There would be others who could care for our parents, he insisted. And they were beautifully cared for in Covenant Retirement Communities in California and Illinois. This same man, so busy with his own work and the Lord's work, had time to remember our widowed mothers with dinner treats and Christmas floral pieces.

One time he learned that a Chinese pastor friend of Willard had arrived in Chicago from Hong Kong. Pastor Cheung was to minister at the Chinese Christian Union Church in Chinatown. His four daughters had attended one day of public school in the inner city and were so frightened by the minority treatment they received that they determined never to go to school again.

"That's no problem," said Paul. Turning in his office chair to reach another phone, Paul called North Park Academy and stated, "I'm sending four Chinese girls to the academy in the care of Willard Grant. Have all dealings with him and send the bills to me." With that simple statement, he (and some of his friends) provided education at North Park Academy and College for these four young ladies.

Paul always discouraged any ideas anyone might have about us having motor homes or a real home. "All liabilities, not assets, in your work." When our ministry became incorporated, he watched others provide buildings at a headquarters base in Kansas. As a member of our advisory board, he was able to attend only one meeting. He chided us saying, "You always know what you want before a meeting, and the board okays it."

"No, no, no," we disagreed. "We do what the Lord tells us to do through the suggestions of the board." To this he agreed after the all-day session was over. "Yes," he said, "you have an unusual board. You let us discuss and decide."

Perhaps the people at that meeting whom Paul had not met previously were surprised when he outlined how we personally should divide our giving. Not everyone can tell someone else how and what to give. But we all listened attentively, for here was a man who knew how to give.

Then in the stillness, he announced, "I made Margaret cry once." My heart was answering, "Not once, Paul, but many times. Once in sadness, but a multitude of times in gratitude."

The last building at our headquarters base is a three-bay garage to house ministry vehicles. It bears the name "Brandel Building," given by three families to honor the one who kept wheels rolling under us for more than thirty years.

ONE OF GOD'S GIANTS

WALLY LINDSKOOG

Wally Lindskoog is a cattle breeder and the owner of Arlinda Holsteins, Turlock, California.

I remember attending a meeting where a certain Covenant lawyer from the Chicago area gave his personal testimony about his walk with his Lord. The date of this meeting escapes my memory. But his subject I have never forgotten. The three divisions of Paul Brandel's remarks will remain vividly in my memory until I finish my race on earth.

He spoke less than twenty minutes, but he used the time so efficiently and covered the three divisions so thoroughly that they are impossible to forget. His three points were: your time, your talent, your treasure (including PMA, positive mental attitude, and OPM, other people's money).

Paul related personal experiences that convincingly documented the truth of his convictions. I think that one reason I enjoyed his stewardship talk so much was that I had been giving my testimony on the same subject also. Whenever I was asked to speak at a fund-raising dinner and could not fit it in my schedule, I would suggest Paul. In a great many cases, it turned out that he had already been asked and had suggested me.

It is possible that lay people who are heavy givers to the church can be used by the Holy Spirit to give a message of the great blessings of good stewardship because we live, work, and face the same problems as other church members. The Evangelical Covenant Church was a lay movement from the beginning. Paul and I used to contemplate why we lay people cared so little about our traditions that we turned over most of the decision-making to our clergy.

I believe we had our most heated discussions about whether one of our sister denominations had remained more warmly evangelical than the Covenant. We both agreed that denominations with an emphasis on life rather than creed should amalgamate in order to increase our efficiency and tone down the pharisaical criticism of one another. We also agreed that if these kinds of denominations could see fit to merge, a more balanced total entity would result—thus creating the best possible environment for the Holy Spirit to do his work. We agreed that if that time came, we lay people would do our part to make it happen.

I happen to be a very non-negotiable person regarding the truth of striving for balance, not only in church-related decisions but also in genetic decisions about breeding great bulls at our dairy, and in all business decisions as well. Paul agreed with me that all boards and commissions should have both clergy and lay people on them and not more than one-third clergy, since they always seem to be more influential. We both had a hard time accepting the fact that the Covenant Board of the Ministry could not see the wisdom of welcoming lay people on its board, and we especially questioned its self-imposed immunity by the introduction of apostolic succession into the discussion.

In 1956 I received a call from the nominating committee asking my permission to place my name on the ballot of the Covenant Annual Meeting for the North Park College Board of Directors. Not expecting to be elected, I agreed. Imagine my surprise when I got the vote. This was the beginning of my being together quite often with Covenant leaders like Paul Brandel. It didn't take long for me to sense the call from God in Paul's heart for the needs of sick people and "fully mature" senior adults.

I can still hear him speak convincingly about the Covenant Retirement Communities. "Wally, you go there to live, not to die." He also felt that way about going to our hospitals. "You go there to get well, not to die." Government officials even recognized his expertise in these areas.

I owe Covenant leaders like Paul a great debt of gratitude for their endless patience with me as I gradually grew from a Covenanter mistrusting of leadership at headquarters to a solid member of the family, recognizing we all have faults and should help each other overcome them. I am almost ashamed to admit that I really believed, when I first started going to Chicago, that Covenant people where I came from were much more evangelical than at Covenant head-quarters and that the further east you went, the "colder" it got. What a relief to find that we are all the same, but express the same truths differently in different places. Thank God I learned some of these lessons while I still had time to change my ways and apologize to people I had judged in error.

After completing five years on the North Park College board, I was elected four times to the Covenant Board of Trustees. Twelve years in this responsibility brought me even more often into Paul's environ. I vividly recall him asking for a few minutes of time at a trustee meeting in which he pleaded that we understand that accept-ing a trustee position at the national level meant that we put the responsibility of the business needs of the Covenant ahead of our businesses at home. God would take care of the needs at home if we would simply concentrate on the needs of the church. "Just put God ahead of your own business, and watch him bless you for it." Paul had a great command of words when the occasion called for it.

The trustee position put me as a liaison to many of the Covenant Benevolent Institutions. It was a pleasure for me to watch Paul gain the total confidence of almost all of the community members on the Emanuel Medical Center board in Turlock. No matter how heated the arguments or how strongly he felt about an issue, he never raised his voice. He knew how to appear like he was always in control.

I still marvel at his ability to visualize what real estate should have an option on it years ahead of time so that the vision he had for the future could be realized. He told me many times, "Wally, take options so you are never stymied in your dreams, but never give options."

God created Paul to excel in mental things rather than physical. We invited the Brandels to stay with us when Arlene and I were vacationing in Maui. We flew from San Francisco and the Brandels from Chicago. They arrived a couple hours ahead of us. Five minutes late bothers me, but two hours didn't faze Paul. I am still amazed that a man who had so many things going could be so patient.

I am the too-frugal kind and had reserved a compact car. With the baggage of all four of us, the only way we could get everything in was for me to let Paul drive, with me sitting in the back with a couple of suitcases on my lap. We made it, but Paul thought I was impossible for not renting a big car. Those who knew him well will recall that he liked big cars.

While staying at the Kaanapoli Plantation, I tried to teach him how to play tennis. This proved to be a mistake because of his lack of coordination. But he was fun to be around nevertheless. If you were dining out, just take Paul along. He always seemed to know the best places to eat. In fact, he at no time expected you to know of a better place than he did. When the better restaurants were crowded, he seemed to belong to the right club to get your needs met perfectly. We had dinner with him at the Nut Tree the night he overate on praline dessert. The next morning he drove to the annual retreat of the western Covenant Retirement Communities in the Lake Tahoe area. It was then that his eyesight gave him a bad scare, and he changed his diet radically to control his diabetes.

I never cease to marvel at the way he made time for the things he deemed important. When the Emanuel Medical Center retreat concluded in Monterey the year I was celebrating my sixtieth birthday, he noticed I was in a hurry to leave. I said I was going to drive down the coast and make a reservation at my favorite motel in an area called Tickle Pink. He thought I was bluffing.

"All right," I retorted, "if you don't believe me, just get in and come along." He and Bernice got in my car, and he told Nils and Lois Axelson and Milton and Rhoda Engebretson to follow. They all inspected the rooms, the view of the ocean, and the restful atmosphere. When we returned to the office, Paul pulled out his datebook, whispered a little to the Axelsons and Engebretsons and turned to the receptionist and said, "Just make that four rooms for those same dates—we are going to have a big party for the bull shipper." I assumed they were joking, but they all came. Can you imagine all these busy leaders coming out for a birthday party for a simple farmer like me? Wow! What a day, what a party! You have to really love people like that. Actions like this not only cause you to care about these people but also to care about the work they're doing.

I believe Paul got the most enjoyment, and teased me the most, about my conviction that flying your own plane makes you so effi-

cient that you get three times more work done. He was determined
to remember the few times he flew with Milt on the Covenant plane
when things didn't work out right because of weather or mechanical
problems. Since he usually had such a positive attitude on other
things, he should have only remembered the many nice, successful
trips they had together. I can still hear him laughing every time the
subject came up. He enjoyed my squirming about this so much that
it wouldn't surprise me if he is enjoying a good laugh in heaven.
I must say this, however; he certainly was ready to go along without
any fear. What a man!

This brings to mind a memory that gives me a good laugh every
time I think about it. The first Bonanza airplane I gave the Covenant was during the time Teddy Anderson was president. (I always
called Theodore W. Anderson "Teddy," and he liked me.) He indicated that he was not afraid to fly in it, but he needed to take a
form of transportation that was more dependable to get him places
on time for his speaking engagements. Trains were the way to go.
The next time President Anderson was to speak in Turlock, of all
places, his train did not arrive until the meeting was over. God certainly has a great sense of humor in helping us keep our thinking
straight.

When I first came to know Paul, he was a partner in J. Emil Anderson & Son, which was owned by A. Harold Anderson. They had
almost a God-given talent for finding real-estate deals they could
do well on financially. They had purchased the Sidney Wanzer &
Sons Dairy, and the farms with the cows came with the deal. I gave
a big laugh. Paul asked what was so funny. I said, "You guys know
how to build buildings at a profit and develop real estate at a profit,
but you are not experienced enough to run a dairy farm." Paul told
me later that this turned out to be true.

He said any advice I could give their manager as to which bulls
to use would be appreciated. I visited their dairy and advised their
herdsman to breed everything in the herd that did not have too
straight a hind leg to my bull, Arlinda Chief. They did not use old
Chief that much but did break Wisconsin state records with Chief's
offspring. They also contracted one of their Pride Admiral daughters
to American Breeders Service, with the sire being Arlinda Chief.
They named the calf S. W. D. Valiant. This bull developed into

one of the all-time greats in the registered Holstein business. The national magazine *Holstein World* dedicated an entire issue to S. W. D. Valiant, and this was one of the top issues of the magazine. Paul got to see it while he was still here on earth. I thought that was precious timing.

In 1978 Paul thought we ought to develop two bulls together. When it came time to pay for S. W. D.'s half, he gave me a sermon on giving a lot of thought to every business deal so that God always got the best end of it first. He suggested I give half of the two young bulls to Swedish Covenant Hospital, and he would buy those halves from them at a profit for the hospital. This worked out very well for both of us. Paul was surely correct. As Scripture says, give God his part first, and God will make it up to you.

I asked the herdsman at S. W. D. Dairy what he remembers most from his contacts with Paul, and he said Paul was always too busy to talk to him much. This seems to be a criticism that goes with the territory for high-level executives who are constantly in demand.

In my lifetime, Paul was the only person who promised if I joined him in a business venture he would personally see that I had no loss. He always said, "I think this deal has a very good chance of being successful, but the best I can promise is that you will not lose." I wish all my business ventures had had this kind of personal commitment from the promoters. I joined Paul in four ventures. They are not all completed yet, but it appears he knew what he was talking about.

I think Paul was ahead of his time when he suggested years ago that the Covenant set up a separate corporation to handle the unitrusts and gifts of going businesses. Recently the denomination finally accepted Paul's idea and formed the Covenant Trust Company. We are now set up to assure proper management and carry-through for these kinds of gifts to the church. Praise the Lord!

Thanks be to God for the privilege of knowing and working with Paul Brandel—one of God's giants in the stewardship of time, talent, and treasure. I am looking forward to visiting him in heaven.

LIKE PART OF THE FAMILY

KAREN BASICK

*Karen (Spoeri) Basick lives with her family in Posen,
Illinois. She is a member of the Mission Covenant
Church of Blue Island and of the Board of Managers
of the Covenant Children's Home and Family Services,
Princeton, Illinois.*

As a youngster, I was a resident of the Covenant Children's
Home in Princeton, Illinois, for six years.
I first met Paul Brandel one day when the superintendent
of the home, the Rev. Harry J. Ekstam, took several of us kids to
the Edgebrook Covenant Church in Chicago for a Sunday morning service. We sang a couple of songs, and then he told the congregation about the Children's Home and its needs.

After the service, Paul and Vega Brandel treated all of us to lunch
at the Tam O'Shanter Country Club. My first impression of Mr.
Brandel was that he was a soft-spoken, kind man with a warm smile.

During the luncheon, the Brandels were observing some of us girls
to try to decide who would be best suited to accompany them on
a vacation to Florida, Puerto Rico, and the Virgin Islands. They
wanted a companion for their daughter, Carola. Since they didn't
know any of us very well, Mr. Brandel asked Harry Ekstam to choose
a girl he thought would be compatible for their daughter.

I remember Mr. Ekstam calling me into his office and asking me
if I remembered the Brandels. I said I did, and he told me about
the trip they were about to take. He then asked how I would like
to go along as their daughter's companion. I was so excited; it
sounded just too good to be true. There was just one thing that
made this a difficult decision. My sister and brother would be going
home to stay, but I would have to return to the Children's Home
after this vacation. Mr. Ekstam suggested I call my mother in Chicago

and talk it over. After telling her of this fantastic vacation offer and explaining my fears, she assured me I would also get to go home, and she told me not to pass up this wonderful opportunity. When I hung up the phone, I told Harry Ekstam that yes, I would love to go with the Brandels.

A couple of days after I graduated from Logan Junior High School in Princeton, I was put on the train for Chicago. When I arrived at Union Station, Mrs. Brandel was waiting for me. I remember the drive to their home in a beautiful black Cadillac. Then I met Carola and Mr. Brandel after he came home from work. At first I felt a little ill at ease, wondering if I had made the right decision.

That night at supper Mrs. Brandel told me we would go shopping the next day for new clothes for our trip. She had also arranged for me to get my hair permed because she said it was very humid where we were going.

I was so in awe of everything—it seemed like a dream! The next day we did go shopping, and she had me try on some beautiful clothes. If I liked them, she bought them. I felt like Cinderella. Then I got my hair permed and she had her hair done, and we talked with the ladies about our vacation plans. It was all so exciting.

The next day I had my first airplane trip as we flew to Florida. There we visited Mrs. Brandel's parents. By this time, Carola and I were becoming fast friends.

After visiting in Florida a couple of days, we headed down to Puerto Rico, where we stayed in the Caribe Hilton Hotel in San Juan. I had never seen such plush surroundings. In the room was a pineapple with a card that read: "To Karen Spoeri—Compliments of the Management." I was so shocked; how did they know I was there? Mr. Brandel had an amused grin on his face when I looked up after reading the card. He had such a way of making me feel important and that I really mattered. I still have that card.

It was then that the Brandels asked me to call them "Uncle Paul" and "Aunt Vega" and I immediately felt more comfortable, like part of the family. Carola and I went down to the pool shortly after our arrival, but not until Uncle Paul and Aunt Vega had warned us not to stay in the sun too long because of the intense ultraviolet rays.

Paul suggested that Carola and I keep a diary of our trip so we would remember what we had seen and done. In later years I was glad he asked us to do this. I had to write a report on Puerto Rico in my Spanish class in high school, and thanks to the diary of my trip, I received an A+ on my report.

Each day we did some sightseeing. We visited a sugarcane factory, where Uncle Paul urged me to bite into a piece of raw sugarcane. He gave me money to buy souvenirs for my family, and Aunt Vega helped me with my selections.

One day we visited the El Yunque Rain Forest. It was beautiful, and the colors were so vivid. I wandered off from the rest of the group, and when I turned around, the path I had just taken disappeared. I'll never forget the fear I felt at that moment—being lost in a jungle! However, our guide, Hosea, came after me and led me back to our group. I never let them out of my sight again.

We drove around the island and saw how the people lived, from the very poor to the very wealthy. The Brandels pointed out the most historical spots and some not so historical. They made sure I had a great time but also saw to it that I understood all I saw.

After our week in Puerto Rico, we flew to the Virgin Islands, where we stayed in St. Thomas at the Virgin Isle Hotel. Again we toured the island and shopped in the stores. One of the highlights was a ride on a glass-bottom boat. It was like looking down into another world—a beautiful, peaceful, graceful world of coral reefs and tropical fish. This was an education in itself.

Meanwhile, I was sending letters and postcards to my family, telling them about our trip. Toward the end of the two weeks, I remember feeling anxious to get back to see if I would be getting out of the Children's Home as my brother and sister had. Shortly after returning, my mother and stepfather took me home to stay. I had so much to tell them and beautiful souvenirs to give them, thanks to Uncle Paul and Aunt Vega.

Through the years, I've kept in touch with the Brandels. Every now and then they would invite me, along with my family, to come and visit them. They were always so caring and supportive and interested in my life. They came to my wedding in December of 1960. I remember Aunt Vega called on the phone, and we had a very nice talk. When my husband was in the Army, we were stationed in Hanau, Germany. Aunt Vega and Uncle Paul visited us and brought my infant son a silver cup with his name and birthdate engraved on it. They took us out for dinner to a nice restaurant in Frankfurt.

During our visit, I was brave enough to ask Aunt Vega if she thought I had put on any excess weight since the birth of my baby. When she told me the bitter truth, I told her I was hoping the cleaners had shrunk my clothes. When Uncle Paul saw how unhappy I was with the harsh reality of my weight gain, he said he had to lose weight also, so why didn't we have a race?

He told me, "Anytime you go for a cookie or something you shouldn't eat, picture a $100 bill flying in front of it." I told him it wouldn't be fair because I couldn't afford to give him $100. He said he needed to lose for health reasons and this would give him more incentive. Whoever lost fifteen pounds first would win. If I lost my weight first, I would receive a crisp $100 bill. If he lost his weight first, he wouldn't have to give me the money, and he would be healthier.

Well, it worked for me. A year later when we were back in the States, Uncle Paul and Aunt Vega took us out for dinner (us meaning my in-laws too). After the main course, Uncle Paul took a $100 bill out of his wallet and said, "Pass this down to Karen; she's earned it." I was surprised that he had noticed and also that he remembered our wager. He told me he was still struggling with his weight.

I knew the Brandels were busy and always on the go, but we kept in touch, if not by phone through Christmas cards. Uncle Paul always enclosed a check for me to buy something for my children.

When my first marriage was ending, I called Aunt Vega and Uncle Paul to explain things to them. They were very understanding and deeply concerned. I met Aunt Vega downtown one day, and we had a long talk. It meant so much to me to know they cared. I kept in close contact with them during those months so they would know we were all right.

Several years later, I had remarried and had my second child, Michelle. I wanted my husband, Roger, to meet the Brandels, so I invited them over to our apartment for a turkey dinner. At that time we had very little furniture, but I was very happy, and I wanted them to be assured of this.

Naturally I was nervous, hoping everything would be just perfect. Michelle was just a toddler, and they had brought her a beautifully decorated Easter egg with a cute little scene inside. She took a bite out of it before I knew what it was; I was so embarrassed. When we sat down to eat, I guess I was uptight wondering if everything would be okay, when Aunt Vega reached over and accidentally bumped over a glass of water. That broke the tension for me, and I still believe she did that on purpose to put me at ease. Our dinner went well, and we so enjoyed having the Brandels with us.

During this time, Carola was busy going to college, then getting married and having her family, but we kept in contact through Christmas cards and pictures. One summer they invited us to Lake Geneva for lunch. It always felt good being with them and knowing they wanted to stay in touch with us.

It was a sad, sad day when I learned that Aunt Vega had passed away. It was so sudden and unexpected, and I just refused to believe it. I visited Uncle Paul at his office downtown and he told me that Aunt Vega had suffered a cerebral hemorrhage from a ruptured aneurysm.

Uncle Paul continued sending us Christmas cards, but that was the only time we heard from him. Then one day we received an invitation to an open house reception to meet Bernice, his new wife, and then five years later an invitation to their anniversary party.

Just two years ago, I was elected to the Board of Managers of the Princeton Children's Home and Family Services. I have been very fortunate to have been able to go to several of our Covenant churches to talk about the home, then and now, and to express my gratitude to Covenant people for supporting it not only financially but with their prayers.

One of the churches at which I spoke was the Northbrook Covenant Church, where Uncle Paul and Bernice were members. The Rev. Karl Johnson, director of development for the home, asked Paul to be there so he could hear my story. I took the opportunity to thank Uncle Paul publicly for all he had done for me and for the wonderful trip he had taken me on so many years ago—a time I'll never forget. I couldn't remember if I had thanked him as a child, but I certainly hoped I had! I wanted him to know how grateful I was and how much he had meant to me through all these years.

After my talk as we were getting ready to leave, Uncle Paul hugged me and invited me to come and have lunch sometime soon. Paul, Bernice, and I had our picture taken together, and I will always cherish it. Three weeks later, I learned Uncle Paul had passed away. I've been praising God ever since that I had the chance to see him one last time, to thank him for touching my life, and also for the chance to say goodbye.

A SENSE OF THE BROADNESS OF GOD'S KINGDOM

HARRY L. EVANS

*Harry L. Evans, former president of Trinity College
and Trinity Evangelical Divinity School,
is vice-president for development
of the National Coalition Against Pornography, Inc.
He lives in Glendale, California.*

I t is now more than a quarter of a century since I first met Paul
Brandel. I was then chairman of the board of Trinity College
and Trinity Evangelical Divinity School. We were having a din-
ner in honor of Richard Welch, then owner of the land on which
Trinity is now located in Bannockburn, Illinois, at the old Edgewater
Beach Hotel in Chicago.

Paul and his wife were present because of Paul's handling of the
legal aspects governing the tax benefits to Mr. Welch. I was to learn
some years later from Paul himself that he took a late flight for Ft.
Lauderdale that evening and began to figure out the possible price
of the land and the subsequent gift benefits over a specific tax period.
It was typical of Paul and all he carried in his head that when the
final figures were worked out, they were almost to the penny of what
he had calculated during his back-of-the-envelope session on the plane.

All I knew about Paul Brandel was that he was a wealthy and
generous lay leader in The Evangelical Covenant Church. I soon
learned that he was a close friend of Dr. Titus Johnson, veteran
medical missionary and pioneer on the Zaire mission field of the
Free and Covenant denominations. He is another legendary figure
whose life has been separately recounted, but it is interesting that
these two intimate friends, with their brilliance, commitment to God,
and unique personal qualities, found each other to be such stimu-
lating company.

One of the regrets of my life is that I was unable to accompany

Paul Brandel and W. Clement Stone to Zaire while Titus Johnson was still there. We had many problems at Trinity, and I felt it wouldn't look good for me to be away. As time went on, over the eighteen years of my tenure as president, I discovered that the problems would always be there and new ones would continually arise, so I might just as well have gone!

My entrance to the world of this unique philanthropist began when Edward Neteland, dean of Trinity College, suggested we use Paul Brandel as a financial consultant after I came on board as president.

Our first meeting was at the Howard Johnson restaurant on Skokie Highway, where Paul often met colleagues for business breakfasts. Bernice Stege was usually along, taking notes on our meetings. She was his memory as well as a keen-minded businesswoman in her own right. Paul would say, "You fellas get a table at 7:00, and as soon as I'm free I'll come over and join you."

What amazed me most about this man initially was that he always seemed to have time for us. Though he had many friends within the Free Church, he was not a member and could just as well have said, "You have people in your church who can help you; let me name a few." Instead, he gave of himself, his time, his wisdom, and his constant encouragement.

I was introduced to his wry sense of humor when he discovered I was another Norwegian in the crowd. A good Swede, he teased, "Well, you know there is one thing Norway has that Sweden doesn't have." I bit hook, line, and sinker, and said, "What could that be?" And his answer, of course, was, "a good neighbor!" This was not the last time he shared that bit of humor with me.

Another characteristic I noticed was that he seemed, at least outwardly, to be calm in spite of his many involvements and incredible pressures.

Paul was a man who had a deep desire to make his life count. He wanted his money to be used effectively to heal persons and transform society, and he had a sense of the interdependence of all of us together. There were times when I felt he had an intuitive sense of the breadth of God's kingdom. There were other times when I felt he was a bit partisan to the older tradition in which he was reared, that in some ways he prided himself on being a conservative's conservative. Yet his intuition and instincts led him to a wide view of life, society, and the kingdom.

Father Dan Kucera and I discovered this at a couple of dinners we attended at Paul's behest. Dan was then president of Illinois Benedictine College. We marveled together at the breadth of Paul's interests and his support for a variety of humanitarian causes. Yet, he used to say on occasion that the longer our hair grew, the less chance we had for donations from him, which was completely inconsistent with his general record of broad thought. It was difficult to tell whether he was having a little flashback to the rigidity of early training or whether he was just having fun with us.

I never felt that Paul was theologically sophisticated, and yet he was a person of deep insights into spirituality. His views seemed to run the spectrum from a narrow view of what the church ought to be, or what a worship service ought to be, to a widely ecumenical view. I think this is often true of persons seeking to be true to the tradition of their early years but with hearts full of love for all humanity.

I was thirty-five years old when I took the job at Trinity College and Trinity Evangelical Divinity School. It was not so much an honor as it was a position that I was warned could ruin my career. In our search for a president, we were meeting in the office of Harold P. Halleen, president of Bell Savings and Loan. Although I was chairing the meeting, they sent me out for an hour, then brought me back and said, "Harry, you know more about this mess than anybody else. Why don't you take the job?"

One of our key decisions was to get financial advice from Paul Brandel. He was with us through a variety of circumstances. When we had political skirmishes with some of the leadership of the denomination, he was quietly behind the scenes, helping us and giving advice on how to stay out of trouble. Not that he was always so good at that himself!

One year at our general church conference, things were particularly difficult. We were having trouble meeting the summer payroll and needed to borrow. I spent a good deal of that week on the phone with Paul from Green Lake, Wisconsin, and he helped arrange for borrowings until tuition came in. He did this on more than one occasion and in more than one year.

There came a time in the early 1970s when an additional eighty

acres along the tollway to the south of our campus could be purchased for $2,000 an acre. We recognized it as a bargain, but it was
still a lot of money for us, since we were trying to raise money every
summer just to balance the budget by August 31. At one meeting,
Paul suggested that if we enlisted eight people to kick in $10,000
each in loans, he would pick up the other half of the total of
$160,000.

Besides struggling to balance the budget that summer, I kept working on people to come up with $10,000 loans. One person I asked
was Elmer Peterson, a gravel dealer from Denver, Colorado, and
a prince of a man. My heart sank as he told me on the phone that
at his age he didn't think he ought to lend us $10,000.

But he would give it. Before he gave his money, however, he
wanted to fly to Chicago and meet this man Brandel. We made the
arrangements, and one of the first things Paul told him was that
he was a member of the Denver Athletic Club. Elmer was quite
taken back and said, "Why in the world would you, as a Chicagoan,
be a member of the Denver Athletic Club?" "Well," Paul said, "we
have done quite a bit of business out that way," and he proceeded
to talk about some parcels of land in Colorado and to establish rapport, as he was so good at doing, with this gentleman.

Needless to say, we had Elmer Peterson's check before he left town.
As I look back now, I realize that Paul's generous giving of himself
and his time, even picking up the tab for some of these meals, was
sometimes for no other reason than that he liked to see other people get involved in generous giving.

Paul and some of his colleagues were experiencing a lot of pressure
at that time because they were working on the old Tam O'Shanter
Country Club project. Just before I had recruited my eight people
as part of the bargain (and I might add that Paul actually enlisted
one of them—a Free Church man who took care of his cars), I heard
that the land had been sold. I was sick at heart, not only for the
investment of our time but for losing the promise of Paul Brandel
to pick up half to save the land for us. In investigating who had
gotten ahead of us, I discovered that it was Paul himself who had
quietly picked up the land to ice it down for us.

Over a period of years, the value of this land rose enormously.
Along the way a couple of our investors died, and a couple of others
needed the money. Paul bought their shares and ended up with about

three-fourths of the land himself. When the time came for us to make settlement, the people who had loaned their money ended up giving the land along with Paul. At the present land value, it is Paul Brandel who still holds the record, as far as I know, for the most significant and valuable gift ever given to the denomination, and he was not even a member. It is also typical of the reason for his success—he could usually envision what would happen fifteen to twenty years ahead.

How, after all this, do you thank a man from another denomination who has been so helpful to you in the acquisition of both the land your school stands on and then later a second eighty acres? With all of his other advice and kindnesses, these were his most tangible contributions. We decided, during my last years of tenure at the college, that we would honor Paul at one of our major dinners at the Marriott's Lincolnshire Resort. There were something like 500 people in attendance.

We obtained lists of some of Paul's good friends in the Covenant Church and invited them to be present and asked Milton B. Engebretson, then Covenant president, to take part. Stuart Briscoe of Milwaukee gave a message on encouragement, and Bill Hybels of Willow Creek Church commended the college, having been a student there. We also decided that since Bernice was such an important half of their beautiful team, we ought to give them both the best briefcases we could buy, initialed in gold. This we did, making the presentations to them at the banquet. Paul said a few self-deprecating words, and our people felt that at least we had made an attempt to thank the Brandels.

It was also through my friendship with Paul that I became acquainted with the leaders of The Evangelical Covenant Church, who have been so generous and kind to me at all times.

I once asked Paul if he had any regrets about any of his generous giving. He said no. But sooner or later, he added, in some situations he would get a kick in the pants. I asked him if we had ever done that, and he said "not yet," with a big smile. He was alluding to no particular group in his string of charitable adventures but simply attesting to what I have heard from other philanthropists, that occasionally people take them for granted and think they should do more or do it more quickly—and in the way they want it done! The fact is that people with money have special problems to deal with (although in my heart of hearts, I have always been willing to trade their problems for mine!) But Paul handled all of this graciously and philosophically.

Recently a friend of mine was served delicious hot apple pie by the hostess in whose home he and his wife were guests. He said he knew it was bad manners, but he couldn't help but ask, "Did you bake this pie?" Without missing a beat, the hostess said, "No, but I made it possible."

Paul Brandel made possible many things through his generosity, and he stimulated many others to give. I will not soon forget the day he spoke to a laymen's gathering on our campus. He said that all of the men who had Cadillacs in the parking lot should be giving the price of that Cadillac every year to our school. It was hard for people to argue with Paul, because he practiced what he preached.

As I visualize Paul Brandel, I think of his steady speech, his brilliant, incisive mind, his Christian, philosophical view of life, his generosity, the kindness in his tone of voice, his deep desire to be helpful, and his dogmatism on some issues and gentleness on others. I was reminded of him when I came across a statement recently by a beautiful woman named Peace Pilgrim who walked across this country a few years back, spreading her message of peace and love. She describes some of the characteristics of personal transformation in the following list:

SOME SIGNS AND SYMPTOMS OF INNER PEACE
A tendency to think and act spontaneously rather than on fears
    based on past experience.
An unmistakable ability to enjoy each moment.
A loss of interest in judging other people.
A loss of interest in interpreting the actions of others.
A loss of interest in conflict.
A loss of the ability to worry.
Frequent overwhelming episodes of appreciation.
Contented feelings of connectedness with others and nature.
Frequent attacks of smiling.
An increased susceptibility to the love extended by others as
    well as the uncontrollable urge to extend it.

In a recent sermon at All Saints Episcopal Church in Pasadena, California, our pastor told the story of an anthropologist who died and when approaching heaven, asked St. Peter, "As a matter of scientific curiosity, could I visit hell for a little while just to see what's going on there?" St. Peter agreed and ushered him to the lower region. As he was ushered in, he saw a vast table full of succulent foods, and around the table were sitting cadaverous, shadowy persons with their arms in splints. Having had enough of this horrifying sight, he asked to be introduced to heaven. Again, he saw a similar table with beautiful succulent foods of all descriptions. Here the happy-looking, satisfied, smiling people had their arms in splints, but there was one great difference. They had learned that they could feed one another.

Our pastor went on to say that there is "an eternity of difference" when people realize they have to feed each other and care for each other interdependently to be healthy and happy.

It is my deep conviction that Paul was one of God's children who had learned this lesson very well.

UNFINISHED BUSINESS

BERNICE BRANDEL

*Bernice Brandel was a lifelong friend of Paul Brandel,
his office assistant for thirty years, and his wife for the
last eleven years of his life.*

My first recollection of Paul Brandel was as a young people's leader in the Ravenswood Covenant Church of Chicago. I had been confirmed in the Cuyler Covenant Church. After living in Sweden for a year, my family settled near relatives in the Lakeview community and continued to attend Cuyler. When I was about sixteen, my best friend, Evelyn Lundholm, and I visited the young people's group at Ravenswood. We had such a good time that we decided to join a Sunday-school class.

Out of that class we formed the Wastah Club (meaning "good girls"). Today, nearly sixty years later, there are eight of us in the Chicago area and several in other states, and we still meet almost monthly. The young men were organized into two clubs, and these three clubs made up the young people's society of the church.

It was a wonderful, vibrant group of young people, and this was the beginning of some deep and lasting friendships. Often we would all go out together as a group for hot chocolate after the Sunday evening service.

Paul Brandel was a strong leader—not only in the young people's group but in getting us together for our informal times. Paul and Vega Rundquist were dating at that time, and I became close friends with both of them. When they married in 1938, I was a bridesmaid at their wedding. When I married Henry Stege a few years later, Paul was the toastmaster at our wedding.

I was working in the legal department of the Burlington Railroad

in downtown Chicago. After Henry and I built a new home in suburban Barrington, I quit my job because there was much work to
be done on the house.

During those years, we kept in touch with our good friends at
Ravenswood. One day in February 1949, Paul and Vega drove out
to Barrington for a visit. Paul said, "You've worked in a law office.
How would you like to come and help me out for a couple of weeks?
I'm without a secretary."

I said, "Oh, that would be fun. But I'd prefer to work part-time,
maybe three days a week." "That's fine," Paul said. "I need someone right away, and then I'll put an ad in the papers."

The following week I appeared at Paul's office at 111 West Washington Street in downtown Chicago. I was accustomed to a very
organized office at the Burlington Railroad and was astounded to
find the floor littered with files, with additional folders stacked against
the walls. I soon learned that these were pending matters and incomplete cases, all of which required action. The reason for this work
load was the death of Oscar Thonander, who had asked Paul to
share the suite until his son, Robert, finished law school, and these
cases had been turned over to Paul and his partner for completion.

Paul gave only minimal direction, suggesting I familiarize myself
with the files in an attempt to bring order to the office. Paul's law
partner at that time was Gilbert T. Graham, a knowledgeable older
gentleman who was very willing to help me with the procedures
for completing the various cases.

This continued for a while. Paul had so much work that he said,
"Do you think you can work four days?" "Well, I'll try," I said, "but
I haven't seen you interviewing any secretaries." He said, "I haven't
had any time."

I then worked for Paul until I retired, spending thirty years trying to get the office organized, to bring order out of confusion, to
complete the unfinished business. But no matter how much help
we had in the office, this goal was never achieved, because there
was a continual flood of new projects.

But I enjoyed the challenge. I thought Paul was the wisest person
I had ever known, but it was disturbing to me that he paid so little
attention to follow-up. He was a man of vision and ideas, leaving
the particulars to others. Gradually, I came to know his style. He

was not a communicator, and so I attended meetings with him so I could be aware of the entire proceedings of a case. We worked very well together, and I did the work as if it were my own.

He was then vice-president of J. Emil Anderson & Son, Inc. He was seldom in the office but was busy attending meetings with real estate brokers and mortgage lenders, planning and attending zoning hearings, complying with and amending zoning and building ordinances. Many of these meetings took place in New York, where financial corporations had their headquarters.

Paul developed a new type of lease for industrial tenants, in which the property was purchased by J. Emil Anderson & Son, developed specifically for the corporate business, and then leased to the client for a long-term period.

He would arrive at the office like a whirlwind, with pages of phone messages to be answered and usually several appointments waiting. The work for his personal clients included cases of probate, real estate closings, adoptions, income taxes, and miscellaneous litigation. I also learned early on how generous he was. Many clients were never billed, and some received only minimal bills. No church or charitable organization ever received a bill for his work.

Paul's association with J. Emil Anderson & Son had started in the middle 1940s. It began with Paul doing the firm's income tax. J. Emil Anderson was head of the company then, and he thought Paul would be an asset for his son Harold in the management of the company. A. Harold Anderson did a wonderful job of planning, architectural work, and building. The top companies of America wanted him to build their buildings, known as the Cadillac of the industry.

Paul was the realtor. He bought the property and worked out the financing. There was continual buying, selling, and swapping of property. The realtors liked to work with Paul because they knew he would be honest and fair in his dealings. I remember when one of them called and said, "Tam O'Shanter is going on the market next week. I want you to know about it." Paul then put together the pieces of this extensive industrial development.

One interesting experiment was the "boozeless inn." Paul and A. Harold Anderson acquired the Biltmore Terrace in Miami Beach. They decided they would serve no liquor and made the bar into a soda bar. They obtained the services of Ralph Mitchell, who had been with the Billy Graham organization, as chaplain. Eventually, probably because there was no liquor and because of the many people who were given complimentary lodging, it was a losing proposition, and it was then leased to a major hotel chain.

Paul said at one time that "you can buy any real estate from Chicago to Milwaukee and make money on it." But he also knew that this required patience and a sense of timing. When he assembled the farmland for the huge Woodfield Mall shopping center, he would sit in the farmers' kitchens, returning time and again, and drink coffee with them. They could relate to Paul; he was at home with anyone. And eventually they would sell him their property.

As a student, Paul had worked in a bank for two summers and had long had an interest in banking. When he was approached to become a partner in the formation of several Illinois state banks, this led to an entirely new endeavor which would prove useful in the transactions of J. Emil Anderson. Paul became involved in the planning and charter of about ten banks in the area as well as in the ownership of several established banks.

In the late 1960s, Paul started to have problems with his heart. He thought it was time for him to slow down, and it seemed that it would be best for both him and Harold if they would divide the assets. It was not easy to divide, but over a period of several years they worked things out.

Paul called his own business the Paul W. Brandel Enterprises. One reason he was so successful was his special instinct for forecasting trends in real estate values ten and twenty years ahead of time. It was like a game. He loved it. He'd say, "I'll buy this and twenty years from now it will be worth that." Some ventures fell by the wayside, but others blossomed into a financial empire.

Working with Paul for many years was a great learning experience from the first day I walked into his office. I was a conservative who never borrowed money, never took risks. Paul's philosophy was the opposite, although he said he was a conservative who only went into sure things. The vast majority of his speculations were successful. Those that weren't were due to his "expecting without inspecting." Because of his many ventures, it was impossible to keep in close touch with everything. Managers in charge were left making decisions that weren't always in the best interests of the business.

Paul learned the idea of leverage from his father. He was in debt from the time he went into law practice until his death. Sometimes people would say, "I should have bought that property, but I didn't have the money." Paul didn't have the money either. He went to the bank and borrowed it. While teaching a class in business law, he challenged the students to go out and buy a piece of property with no money down. One young man did just that, and was very successful. I always thought Paul went way out on a limb in borrowing. But if things didn't work out one way, he just worked harder to find another solution. He could always figure out an alternative plan. That was his way of life.

Busy as he was, Paul was always available to anyone who sought his advice and came to him for help. He was an excellent counselor and helpful to people in working out their problems. He had an inner warmth and strength, remaining calm in stressful situations, easily taking charge of any confrontation. I never saw him panic. I think his easygoing manner was one of the reasons so many persons felt free to come to him for help.

No one ever came to him with a genuine need for money or help that was turned down. Much of the time he never expected to be repaid, and that is what usually occurred. This never worried Paul. Persons who owed him money were not dunned. If they paid, fine; otherwise, he said he wasn't going to worry, because the Lord would take care of him. His faith never failed him.

At the forefront of Paul's interests were opportunities for service to Covenant work. His contributions to the denomination and especially to Covenant Benevolent Institutions are well-known and are described in other chapters of this book.

Paul was a member of three Covenant churches—Ravenswood, Edgebrook, and Northbrook. He served on various local church boards, but his primary interest was in the Sunday school and youth work. He made himself available to have fun as well as serious discussions with the kids, often taking them to ballgames and on other outings. He helped kids go to camp, and he helped them with their education. He used to give his Sunday school kids silver dollars, and for many years he gave his pastor a car every year.

He was happy to give assistance to any church that asked. When Paul and W. Clement Stone were acquiring St. Luke's Hospital, there was a grand, ornate chapel on the property. "We can't let this beautiful church go to ruin," Paul said, envisioning an inner-city ministry there. He then helped a black Covenant congregation get started in this location. With the enthusiastic Rev. Bill Watts in charge, this congregation became the Gospel Way Evangelical Covenant Church, now located at 81st and Saginaw on the South Side.

Paul had a special interest in missions. He visited missionaries on the field, gave them financial support, supplied equipment, and was available to anyone who sought his counsel. He was instrumental in purchasing short-wave equipment for the missionaries at Quito, Ecuador, and in starting the Theodore W. Anderson School there, for which he received a beautiful plaque. His close friendship with Dr. Titus Johnson went back a long time. He visited him in Africa almost every year and helped support him. Paul was as comfortable in a shack in Zaire as he was in the homes of his friends.

Other involvements that he especially enjoyed over the years included being a Gideon for more than fifty years, a board member of Youth for Christ International, an officer and board member of Religious Heritage of America, a member of the board of trustees of Interlochen Music Academy, a board member of the American Institute of Religion and Health, a founder of the National Council on Youth Leadership, and a board member of The Villages, an organization founded by Karl Menninger for troubled youth.

In October of 1989, I attended the annual awards program of the National Council on Youth Leadership in St. Louis, Missouri. This organization was originated by Lisle Ramsey and Paul to assist outstanding high-school students with scholarships for their college education. A hundred students from around the country were there, and three were chosen to receive Paul W. Brandel Scholarship awards that evening. I am so pleased to know that this will continue year after year.

This organization gave Paul the Flame of Leadership Award in 1985. Along with it was a book of letters with gracious tributes from many people, including nationally known leaders such as Governor James R. Thompson, Ruth and Norman Vincent Peale, Robert Schuller, G. Timothy Johnson, Pat Boone, and Charles W. Colson. Although Paul appreciated the many awards he received through the years, he didn't dwell on them any more than he did his disappointments.

Along the way, of course, there were some disappointments. He went into some ventures that were beyond his financial ability to sustain. He was severely tested when one of his banks went through a crisis. Sometimes he was loyal to people to a point where his vision got cloudy. It's not surprising for a person who believed that "a handshake is a contract" that some people let him down. But he turned the other cheek. I was amazed at how he could attend meetings with people who were not very nice to him, and go on as though everything was fine.

Some years ago, Paul and A. Harold Anderson offered vacant property in suburban Niles to North Park College to relocate the school, with sufficient acreage for expansion. It was an ideal location, but the North Park board responded negatively. To the Central Conference, Paul offered 300 acres for camping and recreational purposes on Lake Como in Wisconsin, with the proposal that the Lake Geneva camp be sold and the proceeds used to build a new camp. This offer was also declined. Never tiring of being a benefactor, two sites were proposed for new Covenant churches—one in Arlington Heights and one in Lake Villa. When the Covenant wasn't interested, the properties were donated to churches of other denominations. Property offered to the Board of Benevolence was always readily accepted, the result of which is a core of Covenant Retirement Communities around the country.

If Paul had any regrets in the last years of his life they were that some institutions didn't accept his gifts. However, he didn't believe in pondering, "If only. . . ." He would say, "He who looks back dies of remorse." And he liked William Allen White's comment, "I am not afraid of tomorrow, for I have seen yesterday and I love today."

Paul's father at one time had assets worth over $1,000,000. When he died, he left only a small life-insurance policy. Paul learned as a young person not to hoard because it can all be lost in five minutes. Only what you give to the Lord really lasts. Another idea remembered from his youth was that "for the Lord's work, you can never receive too many requests."

That is why, during Paul's lifetime, many times he made commitments to give when he didn't have the money. Once he pledged $100,000 to the Covenant, and it had to be paid in six months. He told the story of how he got the money. He received a notice from a life insurance company that a policy would pay him $20,000. He put this aside. He owned a lot in Florida that he tried to sell for $20,000, but there were no buyers. Then all of a sudden he got an offer for $45,000 and sold it. Then he received a bank dividend for about $15,000. The other $20,000 he borrowed.

Paul was always ready to host dinners at clubs and to buy tables at political gatherings and charitable fundraisers, and it was my task to fill the tables with guests. One of the many organizations he belonged to was that of the Chicago Farmers. Anyone who owns a farm or is a working farmer can be a member. They used to have a picnic every year, and Paul hosted many picnics of this large group at both his Picket Fence and Lake Como farms.

When Vega died suddenly in 1970, the shock was deep, and Paul was undecided whether to stay in their home on Longmeadow Road in Winnetka or move to the apartment they had purchased on Sheridan Road. Vega had worked on furnishing the apartment for some time and had almost completed it. Paul placed both places on the market, planning to live in whichever one did not sell readily.

He tried to keep up his schedule, but at times it was very difficult. I remember he had to give a commencement address at a college shortly after Vega's death, and it was not easy. When the house sold, he moved to the apartment for about two years. His friend, Dr. Titus Johnson, home from Africa, shared the apartment for part of this time.

During the years after Vega's death, Paul spent time with Henry and me. He felt comfortable with us and able to relax. He had an apartment in Florida as did we, and we shared dinner and good fellowship on many occasions. One day he told us he was planning to move into a duplex at Covenant Village in Northbrook.

When the plans for a couple to occupy the other half of the duplex did not materialize, he asked if we would like to move in. Henry was a diabetic with circulatory problems and was finding it more difficult to keep our eight acres in good order, with lawn, barn, ponies, and ducks to tend. So after a good deal of discussion, we decided to make the move.

Henry had heart surgery in 1973, and we moved into our duplex in April 1974. Paul moved in that August. While in Florida that winter, Henry's circulatory system worsened, and after exploratory surgery he died in Florida the next spring. This traumatic time in my life was made easier because of Paul's understanding and friendship.

I had continued to be part of the office staff when Paul moved his office from downtown Chicago to Northbrook. By this time, he had turned over most of the normal day-to-day law practice to Rodney Johnson and Grant Erickson so that he could have more time for his charitable pursuits.

Paul and I were married on January 3, 1976. We kept both apartments, known as "his" and "hers," and found it very comfortable and convenient. We had space for family, guests, and relatives from Sweden and made good use of the additional room.

We were both interested in travel, and during the next ten years we visited all of the places we wanted to see but had never had time. We traveled to China three times and to South Korea, Japan, Hong Kong several times, Singapore, Thailand, all of the European countries, Russia, Greece, Turkey, much of South America, including Ecuador, Colombia, Peru, Argentina, and Brazil. Once a year we traveled to Sweden to visit Paul's relatives and mine. We went to Switzerland almost every year, and as members of Lloyd's of London, made annual trips to London to learn more about insurance. We visited Israel, Egypt, Nigeria, Australia, and New Zealand, always planning our next journey.

Our last trip in 1986 was a round-the-world cruise on the *Rotterdam*, where we were able to view the Taj Mahal in India, one of the most beautiful wonders of the world.

Several years ago, we were in Harrod's department store in London. I believe we were going to one of the restaurants, and as we were waiting for the elevator, who should step out but Ruth and Norman Vincent Peale. We arranged to have dinner with them that night. It was an interesting, memorable evening, brought about by a chance meeting in the elevator of a London store.

We knew our years together were limited, so we filled our days with things that were important to us. We were both on the boards of the retirement communities and of other organizations close to our hearts. We had a subscription series to the Lyric Opera and enjoyed inviting friends to share the box with us. We had season tickets to the Coral Ridge Ministries' concert series in Florida and shared these evenings with friends.

We often spent holidays at Carmel, California, and drove up the California coast several times. We had spent part of our honeymoon at Lake Tahoe at Carl and Millie Johanson's apartment, returning many times to that beautiful area. We entertained often and also kept busy with our many business and philanthropic pursuits.

Paul enjoyed his hobbies of collecting stamps and coins. He was always interested in photography. An avid reader, he could not resist a bookstore. He collected chess sets and was given many beautiful artifacts from around the world. It has been my pleasure to give some of these items to the Brandel Lounge at Covenant Village of Northbrook.

At the time of our marriage, we had several days of open house at our duplex, entertaining more than 500 people. One time period was scheduled for business friends, another for our retirement community neighbors, and another for church and other friends of long-standing. Paul was at his best, enjoying every minute immensely. We did the same on our tenth wedding anniversary, and it pleased Paul so much to see old friends and business associates. He had a great time visiting with all of them.

Paul had bypass heart surgery in 1983. He recovered rapidly, and we continued our active lives as before. Every time Paul took a plane, his first action was to take out a pad of paper and start figuring what he had that he could give away. He was forever thinking and forever figuring. His goal was to give away everything by the time he was eighty years old. If he had lived another five years, I believe he would have done just that. He did give away most of his net worth, after making adequate provision for his family.

Paul's daughter, Carola, and her husband, Loren Anderson, live in Sun Prairie, Wisconsin, near Madison. Loren is administrator of the Division of Public and Governmental Relations for the State of Wisconsin, and Carola is a homemaker. Both are active church members. I see them often and feel close to them. Carola and I often take trips together. And I'm a proud grandma to Robert and Kristine, both college students with promising futures. This was Paul's family, and this is my family.

Stewardship was Paul's life's calling. He never talked about one particular spiritual experience where it all began. With him, it was a gradual growing in faith. His prayer life was very private. He witnessed by the way he lived as a Christian, and he always took his Bible with him wherever he went.

Some of his favorite Bible verses were: "Give, and it will be given to you. . . . For the measure you give will be the measure you get back" (Luke 6:38). "For where your treasure is, there will your heart be also" (Matthew 6:21). "Every one to whom much is given, of him will much be required" (Luke 12:48).

We had a satisfying, wonderful life during the years we shared. Paul was a loving, kind, caring, compassionate person. A few weeks before his stroke he slowed down considerably. He canceled a visit to Minneapolis, and I was then able to convince him to see his doctor. The examination indicated no serious problems, and he went on to the degree that he was able. He was never apprehensive. He had a faith that was steady, that never failed. The Lord would provide, even when there were serious problems confronting him.

The day he became ill, he went to a bank board meeting in Barrington, and after I drove there to meet him, we had dinner with Bernice and Tom Buettner in Lake Zurich. As we left the restaurant, Paul suffered a stroke. He died on June 30, 1986, after several days at Swedish Covenant Hospital.

He died the way he had lived, working out his financial statement and enthusiastically planning unconventional ways of giving to God's work.

During all these years of knowing Paul. I learned a very important truth—to give as the Lord has given me. Today, I give with a great deal of joy. It is very important to me to keep Paul's philosophy alive as an inspiration for others and to continue financially what he would have done had he lived. It is something I must do. Paul's life made a difference to me and to so many people and organizations.

His life's work wasn't completed. Every morning I wake up to unfinished business. I pray every day for wisdom, guidance, and direction to give wisely, following the Lord's leading. Paul's work goes on.

Memoirs of
a Good Steward
and Friend

*The following recollections from several associates,
friends, and family are further tribute to Paul
Brandel's accomplishments and contributions.*

Class-Act
Entrepreneurial Process

A. Harold Anderson, *President*
J. Emil Anderson & Son, Inc.
Des Plaines, Illinois

It is a special privilege to be named with the distinguished slate of
people selected to write about Paul Brandel.

Our lives ran on parallel tracks for several years before they inter-
sected by teaming us together in 1945 in a business venture. We
were both members of Covenant churches. We were both deeply
involved in business and church-related interests in the Chicago
area. We both had a special interest in Florida. And we were both
committed to giving to enhance the work of the church, North Park
College, Swedish Covenant Hospital, and to planning and building
retirement centers for The Evangelical Covenant Church.

And so when we formed a special business partnership, we already
knew each other quite well. That business association continued
for about twenty-five years.

Paul had a profound influence on people who were close to him.
It always seemed to me that his success in influencing others arose
out of his deep-seated loyalty to them. If a person became Paul's
friend, it meant friendship for life. This loyalty was almost overwhelming. His nature and psyche were possessed of a rather strong
penchant not only to influence and help people but to control them.
I, of course, was not exempt from that compulsion. But it wasn't

all that bad, because being a person that many have attempted to control but none have succeeded, I survived. And I did benefit considerably from his proddings in matters of business.

His comprehensive acquaintance with class-act entrepreneurial process, coupled with his brilliant mind, made him an associate to appreciate. He was also a person who was firmly committed to Christ and the church. He was an inspiration to me both in my spiritual life as well as a good example of what Christianity is all about in daily life and practice. It is one thing to be an upright person who belongs to a church; it is quite another to be a person for whom the Lord Jesus Christ is his life. That was what made association with Paul such an inspiration. He was an honorable man and an exemplary Christian philanthropist whose integrity was highly respected by business people everywhere.

We ventured into a variety of enterprises together. We acquired acres and acres of land. We bought and sold hotels and motels, banks, farms, and even picked up the Wanzer dairy in the Chicago area. We had a lot of fun amid the struggles of being involved in such a diverse array of enterprises. We learned through it all that the same principles apply no matter what the commodity or type of business. Run a clean operation, eliminate any possibility of pilfering or mismanagement, shave the overhead to a bare minimum, and one will more than likely create a successful venture. For us, it usually was just that.

Paul and I were especially blessed because our wives, Vega and Lorraine, were good friends. They shared our feelings about giving. In fact, they were always encouraging us to give more than we did—both of our time and our resources.

Ultimately, we both had homes on Longmeadow Road in Winnetka, with our properties almost bordering. One beautiful day in May of 1964, when homes everywhere were dressed in a glorious coloration of blossoms and flowers, and our homes were no exception, our wives teamed up to invite Covenant people from the Chicago area to a housewalk through our homes as a benefit for Swedish Covenant Hospital. The lines at both houses were half a block long the whole afternoon. It was so much fun that they did it several more times.

Lorraine and Vega worked well together in various endeavors for many years. Lorraine says, "I dearly loved and respected Vega as a close friend and as a person with whom it was easy to share the joys of our Christian faith. I have also known Bernice for many years and admire her greatly. But because of her extremely busy life, I have not been fortunate enough to have shared much time with her. However, I cherish her as a friend."

Paul and I also found time to engage in a bit of recreation, which helped to strengthen our friendship apart from the busy world of economics and business.

The high ethical principles governing our work enterprises did not always apply while we were playing! We took a few fishing trips together, and it seemed to me that most of the time I was the one who caught the biggest fish. So I became just a bit mystified when we weighed in and compared our catch at the end of the day. His fish always outweighed mine. The mystery was solved, however, when I learned that Paul's idea of a good joke was to fill the mouths of the fish he caught with lead before we weighed them. I tried to pull the same caper on him, but he seemed to have more access to lead than I.

In 1968, we bought the Tam O'Shanter Country Club in Niles, Illinois. When we started playing golf together, I made another interesting and rather remarkable discovery. There are rules by which the game is played by almost everyone who plays golf, and then there were the Brandel rules. Any similarity between the two was purely coincidental. It was there that I was introduced to terms like "mulligan," "gimmie," and other equalizing terms designed to ease the pain and respectably reduce scores to acceptable levels. Paul indeed had a great sense of humor—one that made our leisure times jolly and pleasant experiences, not to be taken too seriously.

I loved Paul. He was a truly great person. I am grateful to God for arranging circumstances and events so that our lives could intersect, thereby making it possible for us to work, build, play, and share the collective fruit of our labors for Christ with other people for the best and most meaningful kind of living.

GROWING UP IN A CHALLENGING ENVIRONMENT

Carola B. Anderson, *Daughter of Paul Brandel*
Sun Prairie, Wisconsin

Growing up with a father who believed in giving his time, talent, and treasure to the Lord was a wonderful and challenging environment in which to live. This belief influenced everything we did as a family.

Traveling was one of his biggest loves. The "cup of coffee and" was a close rival but never quite surpassed it.

The first long trip I remember was in 1948 when I was seven years old. It started in New Orleans with a longshoremen's strike that held our banana freighter in port for a week. The timing was perfect—it was Mardi Gras, and what fun we had.

We finally were able to leave and had a delightful time on the blue seas on our way to Ecuador. Upon arriving at the coast of Esmeraldas, we found the only way to get ashore was in a hand-made dugout canoe paddled by the Indians, because there were no piers or docking facilities. It was a long way down to those canoes from the bridge of the freighter. The ocean was calm that morning or our trip might have become one very long cruise.

We stayed with missionaries in Ecuador, sleeping under mosquito netting and shaking our shoes each morning to avoid being stung by scorpions. From there it was cross country across Ecuador via land rover, canoe, and foot to HCJB radio station of the Andes, and Peru.

I believe it was the appreciation these missionaries showed for our caring enough to come all the way to their remote part of the world to see them that inspired my father's travels to all of the Covenant mission stations worldwide. In addition to Ecuador, he visited Japan, Taiwan, Thailand, Zaire, and Alaska. I was able to accompany my parents to Alaska.

Life with father also meant traveling to many future sites of Covenant retirement communities. Many of these trips were spent developing, promoting, encouraging, and sharing his vision with others so that they, too, could become part of the ministry.

I remember frequent trips to Miami, many meetings with Edward Anderson, and much prayer and planning that resulted in Covenant Palms of Miami. Covenant Palms was developed because of the generosity of these two men and others who shared their vision. This is the community where my three grandparents lived for many wonderful years.

I remember my father as the Sunday-school superintendent at Edgebrook Covenant Church. He was the one who made things interesting by "bringing" Roy Rogers and Trigger to our Sunday school to talk about being a Christian. I remember my dad as our high-school Sunday-school teacher, and he was not afraid to talk about current issues facing teenagers.

He not only spoke about using our time, talent, and treasure for the Lord. He lived it. The talks he gave merely explained what he was doing in his own life and challenged others to do the same. During his last few months, he would occasionally reflect on how we, as Christians, seem to have forgotten that good works with our time, talent, and treasure are an integral part of the Christian walk.

He loved to quote down-home proverbs, and these were sayings he lived by:

"If a string is in a knot, patience will untie it. Patience will do many things, if you only try it."

"Once you start something, you should finish it."

"You are not a failure if you have friends."

"Down in their hearts, wise men know this truth. The only way to help yourself is to help others."

He also liked to tell the story of the chicken and the hog. They were walking along the road one day, when they passed a sign saying, "Ham and eggs, $1." The chicken said to the hog, "Let's go in and have some." "Nothing doing," said the hog. "For you it is just a contribution, but for me it is total commitment."

When I think of my father, I think of a life lived in total commitment to the work of our Lord.

THANKFUL THAT GRANDPA BRANDEL GAVE

Kristine Anderson, *Granddaughter of Paul Brandel*
Bethel College student from Sun Prairie, Wisconsin

Excerpts from a speech given at dedication of Brandel Dining Room at Timber-lee Christian Center:

This dedication service has a very special meaning to me, not only because it honors my grandfather but because of the great impact Timber-lee has had on my life.

To me, Paul Brandel was just plain Grandpa. He was the funny person who dressed up as Santa Claus at Christmastime and handed out presents. He was the one to whom I turned for advice, the one who helped me focus my decisions on what Christ would have me do. As I look at the wonderful artifacts that my Grandma Bernice has given to this camp, I am reminded of all the exciting places we visited.

Actually, it is very right that Grandpa should have a dining room named after him, because he loved to eat good food. Above all, he loved his coffee breaks. I recall when we were driving through Sweden in a van, we would stop every hour and a half to have a coffee break. It was over a cup of coffee that he had his best conversations, and I pray that as folks come to this dining room in the coming years for good food and a good cup of coffee, there will be much sharing.

I am thankful that Grandpa Brandel gave and that his contributions have made possible places like Timber-lee, where people can learn about the Lord Jesus. Over the past four years it has also been a place where my own Christian walk has been nurtured and encouraged. As a counselor, I have seen scores of children find Christ, and my life has been blessed.

Like Grandpa, I am sold on camping. It's hard to put into words what my grandfather and Timber-lee mean to me. But this I know. That person and this place have special meaning to me—because it was at Timber-lee that I saw my wonderful Grandpa for the last time before he died and my heavenly Father called him home to be with him eternally.

Uncompromising Commitment to Excellence

Lewis Collens, *Dean and Professor of Law*
Illinois Institute of Technology, Chicago Kent College of Law

My first memory of Paul Brandel dates back to our 1976 building fund campaign. Paul was chairman, and the way he led that campaign taught me a great deal. He was extraordinarily upbeat, hardworking, and demanding. He wouldn't take no for an answer. If prospective donors said they were reluctant to make pledges because they weren't sure if they could keep them, Paul told them that when he made pledges he wasn't sure how he would pay them either, but he always did. The campaign was brief and successful.

Paul remained active after the campaign, serving as a trustee of the university and as a member of the law school's Board of Overseers. He was generous with his time, his money, and his advice.

One day I received a phone call from Paul inquiring about an applicant to our law school. I told him I would check on this and get back to him. When I reviewed the file and found the applicant did not meet our admission standards, I prepared to give Paul a lecture on the importance of maintaining academic standards. There had been times over the years when generous donors expected preferential treatment for students they wanted admitted. Some of these people would become upset and stop supporting the law school when they found out there could be no special treatment.

I called Paul and told him that, in my view, this person did not qualify for admission. I was about to launch into my lecture when Paul said, "Then I would not want you to admit him; it is important that we maintain academic standards and that the graduates of the school have the ability to become outstanding lawyers." Paul needed no lecture. He understood what the enterprise was about and why he was supporting it and asking others to do so.

In the years following, I marveled at Paul's uncompromising commitment to excellence and at his deep commitment to his church and to people. I feel very fortunate to have known this truly remarkable person. His spirit will continue to live on at this school.

THE HIGH EXPRESSION OF FAITH

John Haggai, *President*
Haggai Institute for Advanced Leadership Training
Atlanta, Georgia

Many years ago, I heard about a lawyer and businessman named Paul Brandel who, after determining a possible profit, took 30 percent of the potential profit and invested it "on the front end" in the Lord's work.

In the mid-1960s, I decided that I had better not keep telling that story unless I knew for sure that the details were correct. So I phoned Paul. Much to my embarrassment, he reminded me that we had met at Founder's Week at Moody Bible Institute after a session where I had spoken.

I asked him if the story I'd been telling about him was correct. He said that it was. So I have told that story all over the world— the story of Paul Brandel investing 30 percent of his income into the Lord's work. But the amazing aspect of this is that he invested the 30 percent before he had any return from the deal itself. This to me is the high expression of faith.

The memory of Paul Brandel's example continues to be an encouragement to me.

A MENTORING RELATIONSHIP

LeRoy M. Johnson, *President*
Covenant Trust Company
Chicago, Illinois

Paul Brandel was a legend in his own time. I knew of him and had met him during my student days at North Park. It wasn't until I returned to North Park College and Theological Seminary as a member of its administration that I really got to know him.

One of my original responsibilities was to work with the Alumni Association. J. William Fredrickson was then director of development and the person to whom I reported. He was particularly concerned that I try to raise the level of commitment to the annual fund from alumni—both in the number of alumni who contributed and in the dollar amount. I thought some type of challenge fund might be the best way to accomplish these goals.

Paul Brandel was well-known even then for the challenges that he would spontaneously put forth, so I called and asked if I could meet with him. That was the beginning of a mentoring relationship that would last for more than twenty years. The concept of challenge funds was and is a continuing tradition at North Park. Paul was often involved as the person who participated in a group of challengers or provided the entire challenge fund himself.

However, it was in the area of planned giving that Paul was to have his greatest influence on me professionally. He was the first person to establish a charitable remainder trust with North Park College. The trust was funded with appreciated real estate, and the charitable remaindermen were North Park College and Theological Seminary and Covenant Benevolent Institutions—two of his favorite charitable interests, along with The Evangelical Covenant Church. That was to be the first of several such planned gifts that he was to establish—a tradition that is being carried on by his widow, Bernice Brandel.

When the concept of a consolidated planned giving office for The Evangelical Covenant Church, Covenant Benevolent Institutions, and North Park was to become a reality, Paul was the logical person to serve as chairman of the operations committee, which, in effect, was our board of directors. He served in that capacity from 1978 until his death in 1986.

Paul was enthusiastic about the benefits of planned giving— both to the donor and to the charitable organizations involved as remaindermen. Over the years, we made calls on prospective donors together, and one of his favorite lines was, "Even if you go bankrupt, the most they can take away from you if you have a charitable remainder trust is four months of payments." Our efforts benefited greatly because Paul demonstrated the concept of planned giving by his own giving and by helping to motivate others to do the same. When we started our consolidated office of Estate Planning Services in 1978, we had known expectancies of $14 million. By the end of 1989, we had distributed over $23 million to Covenant causes and had known expectancies of $110 million. Both Paul and Bernice Brandel have had a lot to do with this success.

To work with Paul was to get used to expecting the unusual approach. Some of my colleagues fretted with me because of his unconventional ways of doing things, indicating "we will never get that." But I knew that if Paul promised something, whether we had it in writing or not, he would deliver all he had promised, if not more. This always proved to be true. He was genuinely generous and committed to the Lord and to that portion of the kingdom known as The Evangelical Covenant Church and all of its ministries.

AN ANGEL TO ONE CHURCH

Norbert E. Johnson, *Senior Pastor*
North Park Covenant Church
Chicago, Illinois

One of the most beautiful, but perhaps least known, chapters in Paul Brandel's life took place in Lafayette, Indiana, where I served from 1953 to 1961.

It was 1959, and our church was bursting at the seams with growth and enthusiasm. Our old building could not accommodate the fresh opportunities that were ours.

After much planning, we decided to relocate and build a new church. Bruce Johnson of our Winnetka, Illinois, Covenant church was selected as our architect. This was his first major building project, and he gave us the best of his creative dreams for our new church building.

When the construction bid came in at about $132,000 without furnishings, our next hurdle was to approach local banks for financing. But since our congregation was small, with only forty-five committed giving units, the banks flatly turned us down, despite the fact that we had nearly $50,000 in our building fund.

Discouraged, we shared our frustration with the architect. Suddenly, Bruce came up with an idea: "Why don't you try my former Sunday-school teacher, Paul Brandel; maybe he will help."

The next part of the story will never be forgotten by those involved. In response to our phone call, Paul invited the chairman of the church, Dr. Paul Stanley, and me to meet with him at his Chicago office the next day. "You must have all of the church's financial records with you when you come," he said.

In those days, it was easier to climb Mt. Everest than get the closely guarded records held by our financial secretary. But we did, and we had them with us for our meeting with Paul. Never did two people feel more insignificant and humble than we did upon entering Paul's prestigious law office in Chicago's Loop.

What Paul wanted to learn first was what kind of stewards we were in the Covenant church of Lafayette. Second, how much faith did we have in our dreams to relocate and build a new church. After an intensive grilling, Paul was convinced we were for real. His word to us, I believe, was both classic and highly unorthodox.

He said, "Get started with what you have if you have faith! And when you've spent the $50,000, call me and I'll tell you what to do next." Paul Stanley and I were charged up on our way back to Lafayette. The next evening we gathered the building committee and said we were going to get started. Our enthusiasm also swept the congregation into giving us the go-ahead.

We started excavating, putting in footings and continuing with the foundation and all attendant utilities until we had spent the $50,000. Then we called Paul and told him what we had done. He said, "Good! I just happen to have a $20,000 check on my desk.

I'll send it at once. Continue building. Go to the banks again and ask for a $60,000 loan."

We followed his advice to the letter. But again the banks turned us down. When Paul's $20,000 was spent, we called again, and this time he sent us $15,000 with the instruction, "Keep building, and go to the bank and ask for $60,000." Again we were turned down.

When the $15,000 was spent, we called Paul and asked what to do. This time he sent us $10,000 (now a total of $45,000 without so much as a signature from the church) and said, "Go to the banks again. This time you'll get a $60,000 loan. They will now be convinced you will build without them if you have to."

Paul was absolutely right. The banks now loaned us the $60,000 we still needed, and by late summer of 1960 we had our beautiful new church.

We invited Paul to be the speaker at our dedication banquet. When I privately expressed my deep gratitude to him for all his great advice and help, he shot back with a marvelous line I'll never forget: "Why shouldn't I help? You're the only church that took all my advice."

The members of the Evangelical Covenant Church of Lafayette who lived through this story would agree, with profound gratitude, that Paul Brandel was God's angel to our church. When all avenues closed, he fired our faith. And then with his own generous dollars, he triggered the financing in an ingenious method I had never heard of before or since. In that congregation, his name is still blessed.

HEEDING PAUL'S ADVICE

Pearl N. Krause, *Resident*
Covenant Village, Northbrook, Illinois

We are sitting together at the kitchen table of Bernice Brandel's Covenant Village home having coffee and *skorpa*. We speak of God's blessings, of the opportunities for service that are ours. And eventually we speak of Paul, of his influence on Bernice's life, of the many times he helped others. Each time we are together, I hear about another person or organization that, because of his generosity, continues in missions of mercy.

Our own first contact with Paul Brandel was made by phone about eighteen years ago. We were at the height of our earning power, and frequently there was some extra money to invest. We had also begun to think seriously about our retirement years. Because my mother lived at Covenant Palms of Miami, we knew that a Covenant Retirement Community would be a good place to live. We wanted Paul's advice.

We made an appointment to meet him one Saturday morning in the Garden Terrace Room of Covenant Village. It was an inspiring and exciting time. He gave us ideas for investments that would give dividends then and in later years. These we followed through on. But his main thrust was that we consider moving into Covenant Village as soon as we reached the age of sixty-two.

In 1980, when I retired after twenty-five years of teaching at Evanston High School, we filled out the application. My husband, Harry, had already retired. Two years later we received a letter at our winter mobile home in Mesa, Arizona, telling us a quadruplex was available. Would we like to have it? We returned to Northbrook, sold our home here, and on July 7, 1982, became Covenant Village residents.

We heeded Paul's advice. Now, seven years later, we realize it was one of the best decisions we have ever made. We look forward to many more years of living in a place where there is caring, security, and a sense of family.

A RARE COMBINATION OF BUSINESSMAN-APOSTLE

(Most Rev.) Daniel W. Kucera, O.S.B., *Archbishop of Dubuque*
Dubuque, Iowa

The first time I met Paul, I felt I had known him for many years. His peaceful countenance and smiling eyes communicated a trusting personality. I felt that here was a man who understood himself and, most notably, his relationship to God.

My initial encounter with him came through Illinois Benedictine College and our first attempt at a multimillion-dollar capital campaign. Paul was one of our first donors, and he responded in a simple, unobtrusive way.

An honorary degree from Illinois Benedictine College, exchanges with college trustees, and occasional letters and social engagements were ways in which I was able to keep in touch with him. I especially enjoyed hearing about his travels to the mission fields of his denomination. What a rare combination of businessman-apostle!

Paul lived his religious beliefs, and in that sense his works were powerful sermons. Love of neighbor as a corollary of the first commandment, love of God, was woven into the very fabric of his being. He lived the Gospel.

He was an honest businessman, astute, risk-oriented, ready to piece together exciting and successful business ventures. But business success paled in comparison to his philanthropic and religious activities. The world needs genuine, God-fearing heroes. In his quiet way, Paul Brandel was such a man.

An Experienced Hand and Generous Heart

Brian J. Ogne, *Executive Director*
Timber-lee Evangelical Free Church Christian Center
East Troy, Wisconsin

Being a part-time resident of the area, Paul Brandel had more than a passing interest in our Camp Willabay over the years. In the late 1960s, it became apparent that we needed a new and larger facility. Land values had been escalating to the point where it was out of the question to consider even a modest increase in adjacent acreage. And so the Willabay administrators were searching for property to which the camp could move.

They finally decided on the 120-acre Trout Valley campground near Elkhorn, Wisconsin. The location was good, but the lack of buildings was a problem—as was the price.

It was at this point that Paul Brandel became aware of the dilemma. He began meeting with the committee and made a very generous offer. He proposed to buy Trout Valley from its owners, trade it for the Willabay property, then assist in financing the balance. He requested that the committee continue to operate Willabay so the property would not become an abandoned eyesore to the community while he went through the process of obtaining permits to proceed with development.

The Willabay administrators made plans to move to Trout Valley in 1970. Paul had some difficulty getting the necessary permits, and it turned out that Willabay operated for four more years.

About the time of the projected move to Trout Valley, the camp administration became aware, from an associate of Paul's, of the availability of a 500-acre campground fifteen miles from Trout Valley. The location was excellent, and there were nearly fifty buildings on the property. It had been built in the 1960s by the Hull House Association of Chicago to provide an outdoors experience for inner-city kids. Hull House had decided after two or three years that it was not equipped to conduct this kind of program and put it up for sale in 1970.

The camp administration was convinced that this would be an ideal location, but the price was out of the question. Paul Brandel had been the answer before, so why not go back and see him again. And, yes, he had a suggestion. Now this could become a three-way deal. Paul would buy the Trout Valley property, trade it for the Willabay camp, and the camp board could use the equity from Trout Valley toward the purchase of the Hull House property. But what about the astronomical balance? Enter Paul Brandel again, who arranged for the financing.

Many meetings were held by the parties involved in these transactions, and much frustration was experienced, but the current board of Timber-lee Christian Center (the new name of the Hull House property) and the scope and effectiveness of the ministries attest to the wisdom of the move.

It would not have been possible without Paul Brandel's experienced hand and generous heart.

LOVE, KINDNESS, AND TRUST

Lisle M. Ramsey, *CEO and Chairman of the Board*
Lisle Ramsey, Inc. (photography management consultants)
St. Louis, Missouri

It would be difficult to count the many ways Paul Brandel affected my life over the twenty years I knew him and experienced his wisdom. However, the number-one way he affected my life was to expand my horizons on stewardship. Paul would tell me, "I really enjoy seeing the excitement you feel when you give more."

The tithe was not enough for him. He was committed to investing one-third of his time, talent, and treasure. And there is no doubt, he was an astute investor. His measurement of performance was always a good return, whether it be for a profit or non-profit venture.

Paul and I attended a luncheon one Saturday at which contributions to a certain project were requested. During a break I expressed my reservations to Paul about whether a gift to this organization would be a wise investment. I did not wish to oppose the project, but I seriously questioned if there would be a positive return.

I sensed that Paul did not agree with my assessment. However, he immediately remarked, "You may want to practice a technique a Chicago millionaire uses when he lacks enthusiasm for a request for contributions." I was eager to learn such a success technique, so I quickly replied, "I'm interested."

Paul said, "He's the first to give and usually publicly announces a $1,000 gift." I took the suggestion and did write a check, although limiting my investment. Paul's counsel was, "If the project does get off the ground, you can make a large gift later." His evaluation was better than mine, and later I did make a further contribution.

Paul was not only a master investor, he was also a master in practicing kindness. In board and committee meetings, he was often the last to speak. He encouraged others to express themselves first, often asking thought-provoking questions, something I now practice with my own clients and staff.

My wife, Mary, and I traveled with Bernice and Paul through Australia and New Zealand. He was quick to talk to people we met.

His comments were positive, his actions courteous. One of the things I remember most about the trip was that we never kept score of who paid for what. Paul was not a person who kept tallies.

Paul also taught me to be more trusting of people. It's true that most people are honest. If you give love, you will get love in return. Now I don't recall Paul ever making such a statement. However, when I think of him, I think of love, kindness, and trust. Paul's body language and actions often spoke more than his words. That is why he made such an impact on my life.

AN ENTHUSIASTIC OUTDOORSMAN

O. Theodore Roberg, Jr., M.D.
Chicago, Illinois

The yearly trips Paul and I made at summer's end for more than two decades to northern Wisconsin and the Upper Peninsula were an opportunity for Paul to return to a setting similar in texture and subtle beauty to his ancestral Värmland.

We traveled together by Jeep and canoe in an often adventurous pursuit of the elusive brook trout. We followed streams and fished in ponds created by beaver dams over which we climbed and pulled our canoe.

One evening our four-wheeled Jeep took the wrong route in our search for a distant lake and became mired in deep mud. A tow truck extracted us at midnight after we had walked in the dark and rain and were brought to Watersmeet by a passing fisherman. There is an oil painting in our home by our son of Paul and me standing at the shore of the lake we missed that night.

In later years, this annual vacation included our wives, and although we continued to hike and fish and photograph together, our activities expanded to include visits and dinners at our resort and at the homes of friends and Paul's daughter, Carola, and her family.

Against this background, we saw Paul as an enthusiastic outdoorsman and as a devoted husband, father, grandfather, and friend, whom we continue to hold affectionately in memory.

A LEADING CITIZEN AMONG THE GIVERS

Murray Ross, *President*
Canine Film Corporation
Ocala, Florida

Paul W. Brandel was more than an attorney, more than a real-estate developer, and more than a leader and unselfish giver to his church. He was first and foremost an intelligent human being whose integrity and love shown brightly through every transaction in which he was involved.

I first met Paul in 1979 when we planned together to acquire a retirement complex at Ocala, Florida. It was a very complicated package, and before Paul arrived on the scene, negotiations were in shambles. He took charge in his quiet, intelligent manner, and within an hour the sellers and the bank were on track. He cut to the heart of the matter and inspired trust and confidence almost instantly. Over the next six years, Paul was my partner and friend.

We are Jewish, and Paul graciously attended the confirmation of two of my daughters at the Ocala synagogue. I remember him wearing a yarmulke as he sat with Bernice among the congregation. My wife remarked that "Paul is truly a man of God."

The wisdom he imparted to me about raising my children was both practical and prophetic. He would say, "You have four daughters. Chances are you will have a problem with at least one." He was right, and he helped us to advise her, and she has turned out very well.

The existence and continuation of a civilized world is in some ways determined by those who support its charities. Paul was able to contribute so much because he had a very productive career and used his experience to assist those in need. He was willing to take the initiative necessary to help. He was a leading citizen among the givers.

Beyond all spheres of public and private tasks lies the region of the soul. Here an individual understands the real origin and purpose of his life. To Paul, this understanding was identical with the tradition of his beloved Evangelical Covenant Church. The jobs and titles he held were prized not so much as personal honors but rather as means for giving. He realized that we are here by God's will and that our mission consists of carrying out God's purposes, not our own. There is no one I have ever known who understood this more completely than Paul Brandel.

FRIENDS THROUGH HARD TIMES AND GOOD TIMES

Carl A. Schoeneberger, *Retired Attorney*
Chicago, Illinois

It was the depths of the Great Depression. I was renting a small office from attorney William Scherwat at 188 West Randolph Street in downtown Chicago, paying $15 per month. It was here that I had the good fortune of meeting Paul Brandel, a law clerk for an established lawyer who was a tenant in one of the larger offices.

In 1934, Paul, another young lawyer, and I together rented an office from Bill Scherwat with one desk for the three of us. Our cases were very few and our income meager. We averaged about $10 net per week for years. But Paul and I became close friends as we worked together on our few cases. The situation was so bad that, as Paul later recalled, we each had our own locks on the telephone dials to prevent others from using our phones in our absence. When one of us had an appointment with a client, the other two would step out of the office.

The economy was so bleak that my friend Paul, who had to support himself and his dear widowed mother, once had to borrow a small sum from me, which he later repaid when business improved.

In 1935 Paul and I were working together on a case involving some real estate in Florida. We decided to drive to Miami and invite three friends to ride along. We drove in an old car non-stop, since we couldn't afford overnight lodging. When we arrived, we met with the attorney for the opposing side. Fortunately, all three lawyers exercised common sense and agreed to settle the case without court litigation. This enabled us to enjoy a week's vacation. I remember that we met some lovely girls, and that one afternoon we went fishing. The ocean was very rough, and most of us got seasick. But we had a wonderful time together, accomplished our mission, and drove safely home.

The lack of legal work left much time on our hands, so much so that Paul and I and another lawyer ventured a small amount of money in renting a small store on the near South Side to operate a carpet-cleaning business. We all worked at washing and drying the rugs. But, sadly, we got cleaned out of business in a short time. Most people couldn't afford to have their carpets cleaned by professionals. With all our degrees, we were certainly professionals!

A few years later, Paul and I were persuaded to try a plastics operation. The field was new with bright prospects. Plastic Santa Clauses, signs, mottos, and other items were molded and sold. But this business, too, failed, and so we continued to emphasize our small individual law practices.

William Scherwat was involved in Republican politics, and we secured petitions and got Paul Brandel's name on the ballot for the office of clerk of the court. I accompanied Paul on the rounds of ward meetings where he spoke about his qualifications. Sad to say, Scherwat's slate of officers failed to win any nominations, and so ended Paul's political ventures.

Paul moved out of our suite in the late 1930s to join attorney Oscar Thonander in his law suite at 111 West Washington Street. In the following years, Paul achieved phenomenal success in his law practice, real estate, banking, and other enterprises.

My family and Paul's remained close friends through the years. At times I rented an office in his suite. He was out of town so much that he kindly suggested that I use his impressive office when conferring with my clients while he was away.

Paul and Vega attended our wedding in 1941. Our daughters, Lynne and Mary, both graduated from North Park Academy, as did the Brandels' daughter, Carola. Lynne and Carola were close friends for many years. Paul and Vega took Carola, Lynne, and Mary on a tour of Alaska in 1959 as a graduation present to them.

Paul told me the girls were so tired that they slept half the time on the train across Alaska. Lynne and Carola also spent a summer working at Pilgrim Pines in New Hampshire, and my wife and I drove out to visit them.

Paul had a deep, abiding faith, and I learned much from him and followed his example, especially in altruism, although on a smaller scale. I have many happy memories of our relationship, during the hard times as well as the good times. We have been richly blessed by God for having known Paul and his family.

A CARING SHEPHERD

Robert Terese and Corinne Owen, *Co-Founders*
The Lambs
Libertyville, Illinois

We first met Paul Brandel at a church Christmas party that was celebrated at The Lambs' restaurant. The restaurant was located in a charming farmhouse in Libertyville. It was a very special place to dine, as it was the first restaurant ever to be operated by mentally retarded men and women.

Paul loved God's "special people" and remarked how well they served their guests and how each one had a warm, happy smile. That evening he asked how he could help our program. We told him we desperately needed to upgrade our water system. Paul said, "Go ahead; do it right, and send me the bill."

The system cost several thousand dollars. Paul did not want any recognition for his gift. Instead, he asked that it be designated in memory of Hugo Carlson, father of a dear and close friend, Robert Carlson.

It pleased Paul that our name, "The Lambs," came from John 21:14, where Jesus said, "feed my lambs." He never saw the mentally retarded as useless people as many in society did in the 1960s. Instead, he saw them as true children of God who displayed God's love and gentle nature. On his many visits to The Lambs, Paul always took time to speak to them and ask how they were doing and if they liked their jobs.

Paul was a caring shepherd who simply did what his Lord asked—he fed our lambs.

AFFECTING PEOPLE IN MEMORABLE WAYS

Chuck Walles, *Vice-President*
Hodgkinson Realty
Chicago, Illinois

On a recent Sunday, my wife, Darlene, and I were sitting in a hotel room in downtown Chicago. We were talking about Paul Brandel and his impact on our lives. From our vantage point many floors up, we could see that Chicago is a giant of a city. Somehow that realization and our conversation about Paul had a certain commonality. Although rather short in stature, Paul was a giant in many ways. His success in business and his philosophy and philanthropy are well known, but he also affected people in memorable, but perhaps not so dramatic, ways.

Darlene's college education was made possible through Paul's generosity and his employing her in his office. As a result, a long friendship began—a friendship that, gratefully, I was privileged to enjoy as well.

One of my first memories of Paul was at our wedding reception. As we were preparing to leave on our honeymoon, Paul shoved a crumpled bill into my pocket and said, "Here's something to buy an ice-cream soda for your honey." I quite naturally soon forgot this incident, and it wasn't until several days later, as we were about to go out for dinner, that I reached into my pocket for the crumpled bill and said to my bride, "Mr. Brandel gave me five bucks to take you out for a soda." When I pulled out the bill, I was astonished to find it was $50. We were grateful. Typically, he had made this gesture quietly and privately.

Once, in a casual conversation with Paul, I mentioned having an interest in going into politics—an interest whetted by youthful enthusiasm and idealism. He could have told me my chances were somewhere between slim and none. Instead he took me along to several rubber-chicken fundraising dinners. It was fun to meet some of the politicos I had read about, but I could see that this was not a life for me and our family. Whatever thoughts I might have had about going into politics were put on the shelf. Somehow, I knew this was what Paul wanted us to see and then come to our own conclusion.

Another time, when faced with making a decision regarding a change in my business association, I asked Paul how important my future associate's religious convictions were. I'll never forget his answer. He told me that although this is an important question, a more important question is, can the person be trusted? This proved extremely helpful in my decision-making process.

I remember Paul not only as a successful entrepreneur, generous philanthropist, and motivational philosopher but as a man who knew God and his Son, Jesus Christ, as Savior and Lord and as one whom I could gratefully and genuinely call a friend.

HELPING PEOPLE BELIEVE IN THEMSELVES

Jim Williams
Williams Development Company
San Rafael, California

I first met Paul Brandel just ten years ago. He extended my "learning years," for which I am most thankful. We were using his creative assistance in developing the office land portion of the Marin Covenant Church's property in San Rafael, hoping this would provide a financial bootstrap for the first phase of our church's building project.

Paul and Bernice were unusually committed to this goal, and I was indeed fortunate to be a part of the process. Our goals were realized when Marin Covenant was able, with a little of our help, to successfully construct phase one of the church building project.

Operating on a careerful of intuition into the motivations of people, Paul told several assembled church leaders, "If you want my help and are willing to give me carte blanche, okay, but I think you can do the job yourselves. The resources are here in this room." With that we were cornered, and it soon became clear that I was to be part of Paul's creative assistance plan.

"If you really want to do this and you can deal with the criticism of some who won't understand, then let's get going." That was one of Paul's sage comments shortly thereafter. The decision was easy, and off we were on our pursuit of positive solutions.

Paul and I became partners in this and then another successful office development project in Marin County. Of course, I had to practically open a branch office in the airport coffee shop to conduct business.

During those few years of knowing, admiring, and partnering with Paul, his unforgettable comments and exhortations, encouragements, and occasional chastisements were an indication of the depth of his thoughtful philosophy of service to others. What an ability to show others their capacity to solve their own problems! Progress has been made in many corners of this land simply because Paul said "you can do it," and got people to believe in themselves.

He enriched my life immeasurably, and, over the years, I know that countless others and their special missions were also enriched.

RAISED IN A LOVING FAMILY

Dorothy Johnson Young, R.N., *Cousin of Paul Brandel*
Evansville, Indiana

Paul was a treasured child, raised in a loving atmosphere by devoted parents. They were part of a nucleus of young Swedish families who settled on Chicago's far South Side prairie and chartered the Auburn Park Swedish Methodist Church. They were active there until they transferred to the Englewood Swedish Mission Covenant Church, where they felt closer to their homeland church's doctrine.

Paul's father, Carl, was a jovial, industrious, enterprising building speculator, and his mother, petite Christine Johnson, was a calm, determined, compassionate young woman whose wish to be a registered nurse was thwarted because she was "too small." They had met at the Union Avenue Swedish Methodist Church, where they had friends who, like themselves, had emigrated from Sweden in the late 1800s.

Raising a family in a religious environment was of primary importance to these young people, as they made their way out of sheer necessity and grit. Deeply mourned was a baby daughter who died in infancy. In 1918, our infant cousin, Katherine Johnson, was lovingly brought into their home when her mother, our Aunt Anna, tragically died in childbirth. The first seven years of her life were spent with the Brandels, filling the void of a lost sibling.

The family traveled to Sweden, the first of many visits for Paul, who quickly became fluent in the language and familiar with Swedish traditions and customs.

A happy, husky little boy with a knack for teasing, Paul discovered the wonder of books at a young age and became an avid reader. My early recollections of his intriguing library were fixed in my mind when Paul, at age nine, allowed me, his little cousin, the privilege of borrowing a book, provided I paid him a nickel. Always the entrepreneur!

Books were his best friends and a baseball and bat unlikely companions. Yet he was an enthusiastic sports fan. Marbles seemed to be the extent of his outdoor gamesmanship, except for swimming, which he learned well during the years his family spent at their Cedar Lake, Indiana, summer cottage.

Most often he was the winner of our board games. Later on, chess was a challenge, mastered quickly and remaining a keen interest. Thus his tremendously beautiful collection of chess sets began.

A year of his youth was spent in Haines City, Florida, at a time when the chief inhabitants were probably reptiles, bugs, and birds. Though Uncle Carl did not achieve speculative success there and brought his family back to Chicago, there is little doubt that the Florida marshland impressed Paul with its vast potential. In later years, his interests in Florida included Covenant Palms of Miami, a comfortable haven for older folks, one of whom was his mother.

The Brandels settled in the Ravenswood community in Chicago, an easy commute for Paul to North Park Academy and North Park Junior College. Ravenswood Covenant Church was their church home, and it was here that Paul was confirmed and later married the youth organization's social committee co-chairman, Vega Rundquist.

The Depression struck prematurely in our homes, with the building industry an early casualty. Family income priority was food. This did not deter Paul. He worked as an attorney's clerk by day, attending Kent College of Law at night. It was a very strenuous schedule, with little sleep, much studying, yet no complaints.

The Brandels moved from a big house to an apartment on North Springfield Avenue. One Monday morning in early October 1933, Paul's father, always a loving tease, kissed Christine and said. "Goodbye, Kishty" (his beloved nickname for her). "I'm going to church, and I'm not coming back." Before noon, she answered the doorbell. The pastor and a church member brought the very sad message: Uncle Carl, while doing repairs in the church, had collapsed and died.

Even in shocking grief, Paul's caring and compassion led him to pick up the reins and lead on, providing for his mother for the remainder of her life. Paul had taken the state bar examination that summer. Within days of his father's death, the results of that grueling test arrived—he had successfully passed the exam on his first try, coinciding with his twenty-first birthday. In what should have been a time of jubilation, there was bereavement and the sad footnote: his proud father never knew it.

These are a few of my recollections of Paul's youth. To have shared Paul's life was a treasured blessing for my family and me.

APPENDIX

HONORS AND AWARDS TO PAUL W. BRANDEL

In chronological order

Certificate of Appreciation: Covenant Board of Benevolence, Swedish Covenant Hospital, and Home of Mercy, October 18, 1958.

Centennial Award for Distinguished Service: Wheaton College, June 13, 1960.

Tribute of Appreciation: Swedish Covenant Hospital, 1961.

Plaque of Appreciation: Covenant Board of Benevolence, Covenant Palms, Swedish Covenant Hospital, and Covenant Home, December 5, 1961.

Resolution of Appreciation: Covenant Palms Board of Managers, December 5, 1961.

Distinguished Service Award: Board of Directors, North Park College and Theological Seminary, June 11, 1962.

Distinguished Alumnus Award: North Park Alumni Association, June 13, 1964.

Certificate of Appreciation for Service as Board Chairman: Covenant Board of Benevolence, November 7, 1964.

Plaque of Appreciation for Christian Stewardship: Theodore W. Anderson School, Quito, Ecuador, May 20, 1965.

Honorary Doctor of Laws Degree: Trinity College and Trinity Evangelical Divinity School, June 4, 1965.

Recognition of Generous Support: Presidents Club, North Park College, June 30, 1968.

Recognition of Service: Alice Lloyd College and Caney Creek Community Center, Inc., Pippa Passes, Kentucky, May 24, 1970.

Bell Ringers' Award for Leadership as General Chairman: The Salvation Army, Christmas, 1970.

Plaque of Appreciation: The Dairy Shrine Club, February 19, 1971.

Fellow of the Chicago Kent Honor Council: Chicago Kent College of Law, April 30, 1971.

Award for Distinguished Member of Leadership Club: Illinois Benedictine College, 1972.

Plaque of Appreciation: College of Lake County, April 30, 1972.

Honorary Doctor of Literature and Laws Degree: The College of Emporia, May 20, 1972.

Recognition for Outstanding Service as Board Chairman of Swedish Covenant Hospital: Chicago Medical Society, North Shore Branch, May 1, 1973.

Honorary Doctor of Laws Degree: North Park College and Theological Seminary, May 27, 1973.

Recognition of Generous Support: Covenant Palms of Miami, February 15, 1974.

Honorary Doctor of Laws Degree: Illinois Benedictine College, May 19, 1974.

Recognition for Establishment of Endowed Chair in Nursing: North Park College, May 25, 1974.

Plaque of Appreciation, Giving for Growing Campaign: The Evangelical Covenant Church of America, June 15, 1975.

Recognition of Outstanding Leadership: Residents' Advisory Council, The Samarkand, October 9, 1976.

Recognition as a Member of Covenant Executive Board 1971-1977: The Evangelical Covenant Church of America, June 10, 1977.

Churchman of the Year Award: Religious Heritage of America, Inc., October 31, 1977.

Distinguished Service Award: Alumni Association, Chicago Kent College of Law, June 15, 1978.

Plaque of Appreciation: Leadership Club, Religious Heritage of America, Inc., 1979.

Commander of the Royal Order of the North Star: His Majesty King Carl XVI Gustaf of Sweden, February 12, 1979.

Tribute of Appreciation: Residents of The Samarkand, July, 1981.

Recognition for Holding Highest Lay Office: The Evangelical Covenant Church and Board of Benevolence, September, 1981.

Recognition of Seventieth Birthday: The Evangelical Covenant Church, September 22, 1981.

Plaque of Appreciation: Board of Trustees, Trinity College and Trinity Evangelical Divinity School, November 13. 1981.

Cupola Club Award, Old Main Preservation Society: North Park College, January, 1982.

Certificate of Appreciation for Service on Board 1972-1982: Covenant Board of Benevolence, June 8, 1982.

Honorary Membership in Recognition of Fifty Years of Service: Alumni Association, Chicago Kent College of Law, April 23, 1983.

Senior Counsellor Award: Illinois State Bar Association, June 24, 1983.

Plaque of Appreciation for Board Service: Swedish Covenant Hospital, November 5, 1983.

Recognition for Service: Limestone College, 1984.

Flame of Leadership Award: National Council on Youth Leadership, Inc., 1984.

Recognition of Contributions and Board Membership: Christian College Consortium, October 16, 1984.

Alumni Medal: Illinois Institute of Technology Alumni Association, September 16, 1986.

Privileged Member: Illinois State Bar Association, June, 1986.

Recognition for Fifty Years of Devoted Service: Centennial Annual Meeting, The Evangelical Covenant Church, June 12, 1986.

Recognition for Fifty Years of Exceptional Service: Covenant Benevolent Institutions, June 12, 1986.

Listing in *Who's Who in the World*, 1970s through 1986: The Marquis Who's Who.

Plaque of Appreciation: The Holmstad Board of Managers and Residents, September 16, 1986.

This drawing, depicting the Covenant institutions where Paul Brandel made his greatest contributions, was presented to him in 1986 in gratitude for "50 years of exceptional service to Covenant Benevolent Institutions."

FAVORITE BIBLE VERSES

Paul Brandel always carried his Bible with him, and he often quoted his favorite Bible verses from memory. Following are some of the verses he quoted most often:

"Give, and it will be given to you; good measure, pressed down, shaken together, running over, will be put into your lap. For the measure you give will be the measure you get back" (Luke 6:38).

"Now faith is the assurance of things hoped for, the conviction of things not seen" (Hebrews 11:1).

"Every one to whom much is given, of him will much be required . . ." (Luke 12:48).

"For where your treasure is, there will your heart be also" (Matthew 6:21).

"Bring the full tithes into the storehouse, that there may be food in my house, and thereby put me to the test, says the Lord of hosts, if I will not open the windows of heaven for you and pour down for you an overflowing blessing" (Malachi 3:10).

"Beware of practicing your piety before men in order to be seen by them; for then you will have no reward from your Father who is in heaven" (Matthew 6:1).

"You have heard that it was said, 'You shall love your neighbor and hate your enemy.' But I say to you, Love your enemies and pray for those who persecute you, so that you may be sons of your Father who is in heaven; for he makes his sun rise on the evil and on the good, and sends rain on the just and on the unjust. For if you love those who love you, what reward have you?" (Matthew 5:43-46).

"He is like a tree planted by streams of water, that yields its fruit in its season, and its leaf does not wither. In all that he does, he prospers" (Psalm 1:3).

FAVORITE QUOTATIONS

Interspersed in Paul Brandel's speeches and in his daily conversations were the following quotations, many of which he carried with him on small index cards:

"Happiness is not so much in having or sharing. We make a living by what we get, but we make a life by what we give" (Norman McQuen).

"No person was ever honored for what he received. Honor has been the reward for what he gave" (Calvin Coolidge).

"Down in their hearts, wise men know this truth. The only way to help yourself is to help others."

"It is a hard rule of life, and I believe a healthy one, that no great plan is ever carried out without meeting and overcoming endless obstacles that come up to try the skill of man's hand, the quality of his courage, and the endurance of his faith" (Donald Douglas).

"Far better it is to dare mighty things, to win glorious triumphs, even though checkered by failure, than to take rank with those poor spirits who neither enjoy much or suffer much, because they live in the gray twilight that knows not victory nor defeat" (Theodore Roosevelt).

"I am not afraid of tomorrow, for I have seen yesterday and I love today" (William Allen White).

"Generosity and philanthropy are not inspired by the extent of your bank account. Unselfishness springs rather from your heart or disposition. Anyone who has not learned the job of contributing when he or she has not a superabundance, he or she is not likely to part with anything, no matter how their bank account may expand" (B.C. Forbes).

"God has given us two hands—one to receive with, and the other to give with. We are not cisterns made for hoarding—we are channels made for sharing" (Billy Graham).

Covenant Benevolent Institutions, Inc.